CALIFORNIA STUDIES IN
URBANIZATION AND
ENVIRONMENTAL DESIGN

WHY ORGANIZERS FAIL

WHY ORGANIZERS FAIL

THE STORY OF A RENT STRIKE

BY HARRY BRILL

UNIVERSITY OF CALIFORNIA
PRESS
Berkeley · Los Angeles · London

1971

University of California Press
Berkeley and Los Angeles
University of California Press, Ltd.
London, England

© *1971 by The Regents of the University of California*

ISBN *0–520–01672–6*
LCCC NO. *76–104103*

Designed by Sandy Jo Greenberg

Printed in The United States of America

To Mike Miller

A Dear Friend and
Brilliant Organizer

CONTENTS

PREFACE

THE OPENING words of this book—"Truth may not be power, but political organization is"—suggest what I think the poor must do to improve their economic and social situation. For all their fiery rhetoric, without effective political organizations they can really do little but beg for help. In this case study I deal with a group of highly committed black militants who in organizing a public housing rent strike attempted to build a strong poor people's organization. They failed badly, primarily because their political behavior was shaped by too many influences that had little to do with the political issues. These influences led them to engage in activities that were largely self-defeating. The behavior of these organizers, however, was by no means idiosyncratic. In my many years of close contact with community organizations, I have observed the operation of very similar behavior patterns, which more often than not produced the same adverse consequences. The chain of events that I describe in this book, then, is one that has occurred in very different settings and in many places.

I share with a growing number of sociologists a deep concern about the drift of events in America and a belief that basic institutional changes are urgently needed. I am convinced that these changes will not be bestowed from above, as gifts, but will be won only through political organizing and struggle at the grassroots. With this in mind, I am not only writing about organizers but addressing them as well. I know that many will not like what I have to say, for I have serious reservations about what they are doing. But they should know that I share their concerns, and very much hope that at least some of them will pause to listen.

For their many helpful comments in reading my manuscript, I am grateful to Bob Blauner, Joel Brooks, Jerry Carlin, Art Liebman, John Spier, Rod Stark, Dave Wellman, and Carl Werthman. To Gene Tanke, and to Grant Barnes of the University of California Press, my thanks for invaluable editorial advice, dispensed with good sense and patience. I am especially indebted to my wife Carol for the considerable amount of time she gave to my manuscript and for the many intelligent things she had to say about it. To Nathan Glazer I owe a special debt for his encouragement and extremely perceptive and helpful comments. I wish I could thank many others by name, but in doing so I would risk revealing the identity of the organizers and several others whom I have written about.

Among those to whom I owe a great deal of gratitude is the director of the OEO legal service program, for whom I served as research director while collecting my data; without his active support for my project this book would not have been possible. To Melvin M. Webber, as director of the Center for Planning and Development Research, I owe my thanks for encouragement and financial support in the preparation of the manuscript for publication.

CHAPTER ONE

INTRODUCTION

TRUTH may not be power, but political organization is. As the grim details of poverty in America have been brought to the attention of the public, many reform-minded citizens have acted as if these revelations were almost sufficient in themselves to set in motion the machinery necessary to correct social abuses. Exposés on poverty conditions have certainly stirred a great deal of public commotion and discussion, which has in turn brought expressions of outrage from many middle-class citizens and organizations. But with few exceptions, even the most enlightened middle-class groups have been unwilling to devote most of their political energies toward achieving major reforms for the poor. They have been too busy with troubles of their own. And at the heart of the problem, those occupying seats of power have commissioned numerous studies and reports on poverty but have done virtually nothing about acting on them.

Increasingly, people are coming to recognize that a major ingredient has been missing from their perceptions of how changes are brought about. That ingredient is power. Generally speaking, reports and studies have not increased the power of the poor. In fact, their relative powerlessness explains not only why they have been unable to substantially improve their conditions, but largely accounts for their collective misery in the first place. They have been barred from job opportunities by powerful economic institutions, such as certain trade unions and business establishments. In their neighborhoods, they have been at the mercy of landlords who have permitted their homes to deteriorate as they raise rents. Even various publicly sponsored programs, such as urban renewal and highway construction, have hurt the poor by driving them out of their relatively low-rent apartments into more expensive quarters and more congested neighborhoods. The poor, and particularly the black poor, have been ignored, harrassed, and pursued, and this state of affairs has been perpetuated by their lack of power.

To say that the poor must develop political power essentially means that they must build permanent political organizations capable of effective action. To be sure, farm workers have been organizing, welfare rights groups have been moving the establishment, and senior citizens, who presumably represent the most helpless segment of adult society, have been making some headway. On the other hand, th extent to which the poor are actually organized is often exaggerated in the public mind. Occasional dramatic and violent outbursts, particularly in the black ghettos, the role of the publicity oriented media, and the incredibly energetic harassment of certain political groups by various police agencies have combined to suggest a high level of organizing activity. But more often than not a close inspection of these presumably formidable groups reveals paper organizations with very small followings, and leaders who are actually spokesmen rather than organizers. Moreover, many of these spokesmen rarely communicate with their own people. Thanks to the media, their audience is mostly the curious and anxious middle-class public.

In fact, effective poor people's organizations, those whose organizational strength is comparable to their image, are extremely rare. Failure to realize this has promoted the illusion that the power structure is almost invulnerable; if even the well-organized are unable to win major reforms, the rest can only despair. But a hard look at the facts reminds us that though organization building offers no guarantees of success, without an organizational vehicle the road to change will almost certainly be blocked.

The great importance of grass roots organizing for the poor has prompted some researchers into new areas of investigation. One major effort is to identify and evaluate the specific factors that prevent such groups from developing political muscle. Very often, there are serious external roadblocks, including the ruthlessness of powerful opponents. Yet persons experienced in community organization know very well how internal exigencies, such as leaders unwittingly bypassing opportunities to develop effective political programs, can be highly destructive for the organization. This book makes a modest effort to consider the second issue—how factors internal to an organization of poor blacks prevented it from achieving its goals.

Specifically, this is an empirical study of a fourteen-month public housing rent strike organized by four black militants whose political perspectives were influenced by the thoughts and statements of radical blacks with national reputations; these included Malcolm X, whose picture hung on the wall of their office; Stokely Carmichael, who accepted their invitation to speak with an all-black group in the neighborhood; and leaders of the Black Panther Party, with whom some of the organizers maintained informal contact. The organizers of the strike were radical in their long-range goals, militant in their day-to-day strategies, and black nationalist in mood and outlook. I first became acquainted with the organizers when they sought legal assistance from the local OEO legal service program for which I was Research Director. Thereafter, I associated closely with the group for the remainder of the strike. Their organization, the Neighborhood Action Committee (NAC), created a great deal of commotion in the City during this period, but despite the determination and vigor of the organizers, they failed to build an organization and gain concessions from the Housing Authority.

Analyzing why political battles are lost is difficult and complicated. Interestingly enough, another public housing tenant organization in the City simultaneously initiated a rent strike, and forced an allocation of a half-million dollars for extensive renovations. Though neither the Housing Authority nor the City can be described as magnanimous to public housing tenants, they were certainly not invulnerable to political pressure. Closely observing NAC showed that, barring miracles, they never really stood a chance of being successful. I will explore in detail how they organized their campaign and attempt to analyze what went wrong.

Case studies inevitably raise questions about their relevance within a larger framework, and in fact several broad issues have already been raised in this brief discussion. Is the political behavior of the organizers to be reported here characteristic of other black organizers? Or does it appear to more aptly describe political behavior of the poor, regardless of race? Do the effects of their ideological commitments on the character of their political activities have any general significance? Finally, are there any larger lessons to be drawn from this case study? Briefly, though these organizers acted in specific individual ways, they clearly revealed patterns of behavior widely shared among certain groups. These patterns will be described as the account of the rent strike unfolds, and their larger relevance will be taken up in the concluding chapter.

However, there is one major generalization that is

worth discussing now, in order to forestall the inference that the behavior to be described is confined to persons with certain backgrounds. My own experience with community organizations for over two decades has convinced me of the following: whether white or non-white, middle-class or poor, politically moderate or radical, the political behavior of organizers is often motivated by factors having little or nothing to do with the political goals of their organizations. In other words, behavior that has political consequences, though appearing to be politically intended, often is not.

Since organizers are operating within a political arena, they generally explain and justify their behavior as politically expedient, and their opponents, as well as those on the sidelines, tend to make the same interpretation. An extreme example of how this operates is the penchant for labeling as conspiracies social outbursts that in reality were completely unplanned. In such cases, activities having political consequences are assumed to be intended as well. No doubt a political issue may bring together people who perceive similar objective interests, but this is not the same as saying that their daily behavior mainly reflects these initial concerns.

None of this means that political organizers are necessarily behaving irrationally. Like other people, they are social and cultural beings and do not always make a cold political calculation before taking a step. There are three non-political influences that often crucially shape the political behavior of organizers. First, organizers bring into the political arena values and character traits that have been culturally induced. The social styles of middle-class-based organizations, for example, tend to favor moderation. Their organizers often feel awkward and embarrassed playing militant roles. They much prefer reasoned arguments to the use of threats and invective and operate mainly through legitimately defined channels rather than by employing direct action strategies. These leaders generally justify their "middle-of-the-road" behavior as being politically expedient. Often this judgment seems to make good political sense. But just as often an excellent argument could be made for pursuing a militant line of action instead. In these situations, though the organizers still defend their position on the grounds of political utility, we have reason to suspect that what is really prevailing is their commitment to a certain social style.

Second, the unique attributes of individual organizers are important. Some leaders are more perceptive than others. They vary in their ability to gain the confidence of others and to deal with differences of opinion within their organizations. Occasionally, however, organizational tensions are mistakenly attributed to personal clashes, when in fact values and serious political differences are being expressed by the personalities involved. This crucial distinction must be kept in mind when evaluating the character of community groups.

Finally, the character of the organization itself influences the behavior of its leaders and membership. The structure of an organization, though a product of the complex interaction of its participants, takes on an independent character that cannot be readily manipulated even by the leadership, at least not without serious consequences. I have seen community organizations, for example, that have become so cumbersome in their decision-making structure that they have been unable to respond flexibly and swiftly to even the most urgent political events.

The behavior of political organizers, then, regardless of background, cannot be understood only as a response to the norms of political utility. In one sense, this generalization has limited value because it leaves unsettled the question of how this behavior varies among different groups. On the other hand, recognizing the influence of non-utilitarian factors in shaping political events is valuable for understanding the political process. In this particular case study, it is important to realize that apolitical behavior per se on the part of the organizers was not, in itself, unusual or deviant.

If the organizers of NAC, and also the poor in general, share with more affluent community organizations (and their opponents) a tendency toward non-utilitarian political behavior, this by no means suggests that all are on an equal footing. Since the poor have relatively little power, their margin of error is considerably smaller than that of others, including their enemies. Behavioral patterns that are not oriented toward political ends are therefore likely to inflict more damage upon their organizations; they simply cannot afford as many "mistakes."

Nor can the poor depend upon being bailed out of their difficulties by a stroke of luck. Under certain conditions, behavior that is motivated primarily by factors irrelevant to political aims may still coincide with a politically sound course of action. But even in this regard, the more powerful are favored. Agencies and organizations with considerable political power have many more "right tracks" to be on, and so decisions made for all kinds of reasons are still more likely to be politically appropriate and sensible—or at the very least, safe. In one important instance, which will be discussed in another chapter, the rent strike organizers were lucky despite their neglect of careful planning; making political gains does not, after all, always reflect political wisdom. However, in the long run, neither these particular organizers nor the poor in general can depend upon surviving the consequences of politically irrelevant behavior.

II

Presentation City, where the rent strike took place,

shares many of the chronic social problems that characterize America's urban centers. Poverty, health, and welfare problems are widespread here, and have been growing worse. Unemployment is very high; the crime rate is rising rapidly; welfare applications are increasing; and major racial disturbances, only a few years ago claimed unthinkable here, can no longer be ignored.

None of this makes Presentation City unusual. As in other cities, the poor and minority groups cluster together, and their problems, frustrations, and reactions fill statistical compendiums and the daily newspapers. What is unique about the City is the ease with which local conditions permit its more fortunate citizens to ignore the really pressing social issues. Though the population approaches one million, many urban problems commonly associated with high density are fairly minimal. Traffic within the City is generally not as congested as elsewhere, air pollution is relatively low, and the noise level is quite tolerable. The City is skirted by easily accessible recreational areas, and within the City itself there are excellent parks and other recreational facilities. Ask any resident of Presentation City, rich or poor, and he will probably tell you what a great city it is to live in. However, the poor, who have less chance to escape, cannot readily ignore their dire situation. For the middle class, on the other hand, the City's favorable conditions make it easier to forget about the poor.

For example, consider the housing of the poor. The dingy blacks and greys of most residential structures in other cities are virtually absent here. The physical problems that ail housing in Presentation City, which are considerable, are hidden beneath a cheerful, light-colored façade. Tourists remark that the whole town appears recently painted, and many residents still believe that there are virtually no slums in the City.

Appearances are deceiving, however; vast sections of Presentation City could fairly be called pastel slums. Though most residents would resent such a description, on this score the City's poor and many public officials agree. The Department of Building Inspection admits that unsanitary and unsafe conditions are extensive in the poorer residential areas. In fact, the Department of City Planning provides maps delineating the vast sections of the City containing structures regarded as physically deteriorated.

The poor have been able to do little or nothing to compel landlords or public enforcement agencies to bring these buildings up to adequate safety and health standards. When tenants complain to housing inspectors, they rarely receive anything better than minor changes. And there is always the danger that contacting an inspector will lead the landlord to retaliate by evicting tenants or raising rents. Then too, sincere inspectors sometimes find themselves forced to recommend demolition rather than repair. In short, tenants who complain generally have little to gain but a great deal to lose.

In theory, and sometimes in practice, there are public agencies that acknowledge their responsibility to tenants residing in private housing. This is not so for public housing tenants. The Department of Building Inspection, which is responsible for seeing that private housing meets code standards, regards public housing as off base; its administrators claim that one public agency has no business supervising the activities of another. Public housing tenants have repeatedly complained to them, but in vain.

Individual tenants can do little but deal directly with the Housing Authority. Though accounts of the problems of the poor confronting an elaborate bureaucratic maze are legend, tenants of the City's Housing Authority are spared the anxiety of the sort of runaround that their encounters with large-scale public agencies often involve. Tenants with complaints simply appear in person or call the office located at their project. Whether to replace a window, repair plumbing, or fix a leaky roof, the procedure is the same, and the local office submits the complaint to the maintenance department. However, the absence of red tape is not necessarily a blessing; the channels of communication are relatively direct and clear, but they still often lead to few results or none at all.

At the Rogers Point Project, where the rent strike occurred, tenants and the Housing Authority have clashed over the length of time it takes for repairs to be made. A plumbing stoppage, for example, is generally handled within two days after tenants complain. For the Housing Authority, with its small maintenance staff, this seems a reasonable waiting period; it can hardly be so for the tenants. Other grievances take much longer to satisfy. Broken windows, which are almost immediately boarded with wooden planks, are not usually replaced with regular window panes for several months. Still other complaints are not answered at all. For example, faulty but still operative refrigerators generally are neither repaired nor replaced, and complaints of tilted stoves, which cause pots and pans to slide off, go unheeded. A common tenant grievance is that apartments are never painted. Actually they are painted on the average of every ten years; thus only a long-term tenant is likely to live in one that is freshly done, and even they complain that a ten-year time lag is far too long.

Inadequate responses to tenant complaints are serious enough, but there is a more basic problem. The Rogers Point Project is progressively deteriorating physically, and the process seems irreversible. Most of its units were built in 1941, which makes the project the second oldest in the City. For tenants, the issue is not only poor handling of complaints, but the fact they have so many in the first place. In fact, from 1963 to 1967, complaints to the Housing Authority increased more than 50 per cent. Perhaps tenants have become more conscious of their rights and are willing to express them. But according to the Housing Authority, this rise reflects budgetary limitations originally imposed upon its maintenance program. The Housing Authority was budgeted to make only what are called "normal repairs." Neither the City nor the federal government at that time contributed funds to cope with obsolescence. Essentially, the federal government finances the building of public housing but not its regular operation. The Housing Authority is supposed to finance its operation with funds collected from rents. This makes it impossible for the agency to make more than normal repairs without raising rents or obtaining subsidies. With the Housing Authority unable to cope with the costs of obsolescence, the structures at Rogers Point have continued to deteriorate. Hence more complaints.

One tragic example of the limitations of making only normal repairs is the occasional breaking of a sewage pipe, which has flooded the project with waste. These pipes should have been replaced long ago, but the Housing Authority has been unable to afford that. In fact, the deterioration resulting from obsolescence, which has affected the older projects most adversely, led the Housing Authority's executive director, John O'Rourke, to request an appropriation of several million dollars from the federal government. He was turned down.

Finally, tenants felt unfairly treated by the Housing Authority. For example, they claimed that the agency was unjustly charging them for repairs it mistakenly believed they were responsible for. Tenants whose windows were broken had to pay the cost of replacing them, no matter who was to blame for the damage. The Housing Authority argued that tenants share collective responsibility. Tenants also complained that staff members treated them discourteously, which further confirmed their belief that the Housing Authority was completely unconcerned with their welfare. The gap that developed between what tenants believed they deserve and what the Housing Authority actually offered generated considerable hostility among tenants, and made at least some of them amenable to engaging in protest activities.

III

The Housing Authority reformed some of its practices and policies in response to the many grievances that tenants expressed, but on the whole conditions remained about the same. The constant tenant irritation over housing conditions was one important factor that made a fourteen-month rent strike against the Housing Authority possible; but tenant dissatisfaction alone could not have accounted for the ability to wage so long a war against the agency.

Significantly, no striking tenants were ever evicted, nor were the organizers forced by the Housing Authority and the courts to cease their activities. What is more, the organizers were on the public payroll—employed by the City's poverty program—and in fact conducted the affairs of the rent strike not off the job but in their official capacity. They even used the facilities of the poverty program to conduct the strike. Had they lost their positions or been restrained, strike activities would have been very difficult to carry on. But the organizers remained fairly secure in their jobs and operated with considerable latitude.

It was rumored around the City that high-echelon poverty executives were really behind the strike. Those more intimately familiar with the politics of the City's poverty program knew that this was not so. The poverty program administrators were receptive to new ideas, but rent strikes were not the kind of social experiment that they had in mind. They believed that maintaining close ties with the official establishment was important to carrying out their various programs. Not least important, they were antagonistic to any proposal that could threaten the funding of the poverty program.

How was it possible, then, for the tenants and organizers to continue their disruptive activities with a minimal amount of intrusion from poverty program officials? And why didn't the Housing Authority and its allies take strong measures against the tenants and the organizers? To answer these questions, we shall look at three important events. First was the successful battle by neighborhood groups for control of the City's poverty program, which decentralized political decision making and provided greater leverage to those at the very bottom of the political hierarchy. Second, a major confrontation between the Housing Authority and tenants elsewhere in the City led to a moratorium on evictions, which in turn aided the activities of the strike. Third, a power struggle between the strike organizers and their official superiors had a major impact upon the ability of the organizers to conduct their strike in their official capacity and with impunity. I shall take up the first two issues now, and turn to the third one in the next chapter.

As I have said, NAC lost the strike badly, largely because of internal weaknesses. What these weaknesses were will begin to become clear in the discussion of the various battles the organizers had with their superiors in the poverty program, battles from which they emerged victorious. In subsequent chapters, I will discuss how the organizers related to the tenants, the official establishment, and their lawyers. Having witnessed the full scope of their political conduct in relation to the rent strike, we shall be in a position to evaluate the major factors that accounted for their political behavior.

IV

Real power is highly persuasive. But merely convincing others that one has considerable power may sometimes be a suitable substitute, as we can see from the manner in which blacks won political control of the poverty program in Presentation City. Throughout the country, the maximum feasible participation clause of the poverty program opened a political Pandora's box. The poverty act stated that the community action program was to be "developed, conducted, and administered with the maximum feasible participation of the residents and members of the group served." To the mayor of Presentation City, this meant that the poor would be involved as his appointees. Community leaders believed that the neighborhood poor should elect their own representatives. Around this issue a political struggle ensued.

The first stage of the battle, which representatives of the poor thought would be the final, was over in three weeks, when after several public debates and private meetings the mayor conceded control of the poverty program to the neighborhoods. Since the black leadership, though quite vocal, did not have sufficient political leverage to force this decision upon him, it was not altogether clear why he had conceded. Several people close to the mayor claimed that he really did not understand the implications of his decision. Others claimed that he did, and called attention to his liberal record as evidence. What did appear fairly certain was the lack of any strong, organized opposition to neighborhood control.

Community leaders rejoiced over the mayor's decision,

but not for long. After being prevailed upon by two of his associates, one a high-placed labor official and the other a prominent businessman, the mayor decided that he had made a mistake and publicly reversed his decision. Obviously, this was a serious setback for neighborhood groups. But it was better for the community leadership that this occurred in the beginning, rather than not at all, for it tended to increase their moral and political capital; even many who thought that the mayor should retain control of the poverty program believed that he had acted rather shabbily.

The black leaders and their allies thus gained support, but they were still a political minority. Pending the writing and approval of a constitution, all the delegates on the policy-making Economic Opportunity Council were appointed by the mayor. Most of them, not surprisingly, supported his position. What is more, while winning some allies, the blacks were in danger of losing others: two non-black poverty communities, or target areas, as they were officially called, were becoming much more concerned with obtaining federal funds quickly than with achieving community control of the program. Though it was an unlikely prospect, some feared losing the program altogether. And blacks themselves were defecting from the ranks. The president of the provisional Economic Opportunity Council, who was black, had played a cautious role but soon began to pressure his black peers to yield. One very influential black delegate, who had pushed hard for local control, finally capitulated and publicly stated, "People in the target areas do not desire to control the war on poverty. They only want a voice in the decision-making process." This represented a serious crack in the community leadership. Other black leaders began to express willingness to accept a compromise plan that would increase the number of delegates elected to the Economic Opportunity Council while leaving the mayor power to appoint the majority. Apparently, the deadlock was breaking, with only a few of the least influential blacks holding out. And a deadlock it had certainly been, because the federal government required both City Hall approval and community consensus as a condition for releasing funds.

However, on an evening in August of 1965, while the future of Presentation City's poverty program was being debated, police were sealing off, in vain, an eight-block area in the black ghetto of Los Angeles, Watts, in order to contain a blossoming riot. The response by public officials and black leaders to this major disturbance certainly influenced the mayor's decision, his final one this time, to relinquish control of the poverty program to the poor. As elsewhere, the City was fearful that the Los Angeles riot might set off a similar conflagration in Presentation City. In fact, the City's legislative body, the Board of Supervisors, convened to discuss preventive measures, and the mayor alerted the City's protective services. When the mayor publicly stated, "I don't think anybody in any city in the United States can say 'It can't happen here,' " he undoubtedly reflected the prevailing mood of the City.

The mayor was also concerned about the possible impact of the Watts riot upon the battle for control of the poverty program. He had told several associates privately that he feared that black leaders might attempt to capitalize on it. He publicly warned that the riot "should be an inducement to get the show on the road," but added that "it should not be used as a wedge for these people to move in and get their own way." His anxieties were well founded. The Watts riot swiftly healed the rift between the many who were willing to accept City Hall's compromise plan and the few who would not. It was settled in favor of the few. These black leaders actually had no substantial community base of their own with which to badger the establishment. Several of them quite effectively described to others the plight of the poor blacks, but organizationally speaking, they did not really represent them. Yet even without a constituency, they were able to gain considerable political confidence from an event that had occurred elsewhere, one which was beyond their control. The mayor pleaded that the Watts riot not be used as a wedge, but the black leadership disagreed. Reunited again, they issued a determined press statement: "At no time will any governing body of the Economic Opportunity Council have less than a simple majority from the target areas."

These community leaders, including those who only days before had been willing to accept the compromise solution, began making public statements on the danger of riot in Presentation City. Implied threats were continuously issued. For example, one black spokesman stated, in a rather passionate address to the public, that "fantastic energies seethe among the City's Negroes, and they can explode." At an official meeting of delegates to the poverty program, one of the delegates warned that "if frustrations and energies built up over a century are not channeled in a constructive way, they will surely explode in the manner Watts did." He continued: "There is urgency in this matter. There is grave need for some sign to the people that you are in sympathy." Of course, the message was clear—either transfer control of the poverty program to the poverty communities, or risk the danger of a riot. Not that these leaders would have actually carried through their admonitions by deliberately inciting a riot; this was really not their style of politics. But they did assume that their opponents would be frightened enough to believe that their public remarks might set off a disturbance, and even at the risk that this might conceivably happen, they deliberately pursued the bluff.

One excellent example of this strategy was the calculated risk taken by one black spokesman who threatened a massive demonstration for the following weekend. Actually, only a few of the other leaders supported this tactic, and this particular one privately admitted that he would have been hard pressed to locate even a dozen persons to participate. But he had heard that influential persons in the City, including the mayor, were frightened, and he figured that they would be most unlikely to put his threat to a test.

Bluffing one's political opponents involves great risks, but in this instance the threat of a massive demonstration turned out to be an effective political maneuver. At the next meeting of the Executive Committee of the Economic Opportunity Council, the delegates voted 7-0, with three abstentions, to transfer control of the poverty program to the neighborhoods. Actually, this Committee was only an advisory arm of the Council, and therefore lacked the power to change the constitution. Nevertheless, the vote for neighborhood control was politically significant. Not only was there no opposition; the three who abstained had, until then, been arch, outspoken foes of neighborhood control.

The spokesman who had threatened a mass demonstration announced that on the basis of the Committee's vote, the demonstration would tentatively be called off. He and other leaders would wait to see if the policy-making Economic Opportunity Council would support the position taken by the Executive Committee. In the interim, black leaders lined up citizens and organizations to speak on their behalf at the council. When it convened, over fifty individuals, virtually all representing organizations, spoke in favor of neighborhood control of the poverty program. They came from such diverse sectors of the community as property owners' associations, churches, and social welfare agencies. The following day, after the mayor received reports of the overwhelming testimony in favor of shifting control of the poverty program to the neighborhoods, he finally capitulated to the demands of the target areas.

Specifically, each of the poverty target areas now enjoyed within its own geographical jurisdiction broad powers over initiating and implementing programs and hiring its own personnel, including an executive director. The Economic Opportunity Council could veto programs, but with a majority of delegates to the central body chosen by the neighborhoods rather than by the mayor, this was unlikely to occur. No matter what differences existed between the various target areas, they respected each other's political turf. Furthermore, a two-thirds vote was necessary to overturn a program. So, practically speaking, each poverty jurisdiction pretty much ran its own business.

Various factors, including the political astuteness of the black leaders, widespread community support, and the mayor's own political mistakes contributed to the successful political battle for neighborhood control. Support eventually came not only from liberal elements but from many conservatives as well. The black leadership repeatedly argued the superiority of self-help programs to eradicate poverty, which neighborhood control would presumably make possible. Some spokesmen offered this as a possible alternative to the welfare model, which they claimed tends to perpetuate the poverty of the poor. Members of the business community and other influential citizens who were critical of traditional welfare programs found their arguments persuasive. Finally, the possibility of riot played a major role.

To the black leaders themselves, what seemed decisive was this last factor—the threat of a major disturbance. Were it not for the coincidental timing of the Watts riot and their own battle with the mayor, they believed the the City would not have conceded. To these leaders around the City, winning control of the program was extremely significant.

The mayor, on numerous occasions, had insisted that he would never give in, but he did. And he did so not because they had organized their potential base, but because in their role as spokesmen, within the context of a very tense situation, they were able to frighten the establishment into submission. The organizers of the rent strike in Rogers Point never forgot this lesson.

V

In the late winter of 1966, John O'Rourke, the newly appointed executive director of the Presentation City Housing Authority, was put to an extremely difficult test. The Housing Authority was processing another routine eviction of a family located in a black ghetto of the City, South Peak. The family had been ordered to leave for non-payment of rent, but they simply ignored the Housing Authority. The agency then proceeded to obtain what is called a writ of possession, which allows the Housing Authority to order the county sheriff to forcibly evict such tenants. When two deputy sheriffs, accompanied by moving men, arrived at South Peak, only the head of the household was home. They entered the apartment to remove the furniture, and received no resistance. However, a neighbor watching the eviction phoned the local poverty office to ask it to intervene. South Peak was one of the several designated poverty target areas in the City which, as a result of winning the political battle against the mayor for neighborhood control, had its own area board, with members elected by the poor residents.

With an area board whose majority resided in public housing, it was not surprising that the South Peak Economic Opportunity Council responded favorably to the phone call. Frank Bates, who was directly responsible for the supervision of the EOC organizers, swiftly mobilized staff members and public housing residents to block the eviction. Had Bates been directly answerable to the downtown office rather than to his own area board, he might not have been so willing to act—at least not if he wished to risk losing his job.

To block the eviction, more than a hundred persons jammed rooms, corridors, and other passageways. The deputy sheriffs, not being able to evict the family, finally returned the furniture to the household and left. The Housing Authority could have ordered the sheriff's department to return with reinforcements. In fact, the agency's executive director, O'Rourke, was urged to do so by several of his high-echelon administrators. They argued that to permit this family to remain would undermine confidence in the Housing Authority, for it would show others that a resisting force could effectively prevail.

O'Rourke, on the other hand, saw this crisis as an opportunity to demonstrate to the tenants and their allies that his agency was not the ogre they imagined but was committed to pursuing policies that were in the tenants' interests. Under his predecessor, the Housing Authority had gained a reputation as an unduly harsh, unfair, and arbitrary landlord. O'Rourke believed that changing this tainted image of the Housing Authority was among his major tasks. After all, tenant outcry, supported by many citizens, had in part accounted for the mayor using his influence to replace the former executive director with a more liberal one. There was an additional political factor: opponents of urban renewal, who were numerous in Presentation City, were claiming that virtually no relocation housing was available. The redevelopment agency maintained that public housing was an adequate resource which would provide displaced residents with decent housing. The image of public housing, then, was a crucial aspect of the City's urban renewal program.

The conciliatory position of the new executive director was officially endorsed by the Housing Authority commissioners. But neither O'Rourke nor the commissioners intended a moratorium on eviction. While agreeing to halt this particular eviction, O'Rourke insisted that the Housing Authority had the right and the duty to evict rent-delinquent tenants. On this score, he agreed with the other administrators. But he also believed that every effort should first be made to establish a good working relationship with the tenants, and also to review alternatives other than eviction for assuring that tenants pay rent. As O'Rourke said: "They can always be evicted. That's easy."

To many citizens around the City, fear of riot was assumed to be the prime factor for backing off on the eviction. Of course, O'Rourke did not want to precipitate a riot, but this was not his main concern. He was appointed chief administrator of the Housing Authority in the first place to improve the image of public housing, and to deal as effectively as possible with tenant grievances. He also had a very liberal conception of the Authority's role. While his predecessor and others viewed the operation of the Housing Authority as essentially a business enterprise, O'Rourke stressed social welfare. He was anxious to work closely with tenants to develop various programs, including, for example, recreational and employment projects. Later he even gave the social work staff the right of approving or disapproving eviction orders. He believed that the circumstances of tenants should be taken into consideration when making important decisions that affected their welfare. This kind of thinking, much more than any fear of riot, accounted for his decision to reverse the eviction order.*

---

* It was interesting to see how the differences between O'Rourke and the hard-line administrators were reflected in the respective positions taken on this issue by the City's two major newspapers. Both the liberal *Post* and the

It turned out, however, that O'Rourke was wrong to assume that his conciliatory posture would encourage a cooperative stance by the tenants and the newly formed South Peak branch of the poverty program. Instead, the organizers believed that the road to reform of the Housing Authority depended upon pursuing a militant course; not less but more pressure must be exerted against the Housing Authority. From their view, it was a militant show of strength in the first place that halted the eviction. As one of the poverty program organizers put it, they had succeeded in scaring the agency "out of its wits." That another Housing Authority administrator would have responded differently to the sit-in was beside the point to them.

At the next Housing Authority commission meeting, more than fifty South Peak residents crowded the small conference room. After the meeting officially closed and the commissioners were preparing to leave, they blocked the doorway to force them to listen to their demands. Only after a long list of grievances was recited did they permit the commissioners to leave. A few days later, organizers employed by the South Peak poverty program put together a City-wide tenant organization, the Presentation City Tenant

---

fairly conservative *Mirror* believed that the Housing Authority had an obligation to act in its own interest, but each defined that self-interest quite differently. The *Post* editorially applauded the Housing Authority's willingness to respond to tenant needs, including its decision to defer the eviction of the family protected by EOC. The *Mirror*, on the other hand, in its editorial entitled "A Firm Stance," stressed the duty of the Housing Authority to evict undesirable tenants. It is not that the *Post* feared a riot and the *Mirror* did not. In fact, an article appeared in the *Mirror* making the observation that a riot had almost occurred as a result of the impending eviction. Ideology, apparently, rather than practical considerations, shaped their different editorial policies. Likewise, Housing Authority administrators opposed to O'Rourke's decision believed that illegitimate force must, on principle, be firmly opposed, regardless of riot risks. To O'Rourke, the Housing Authority was obliged to respond to the legitimate concerns of tenants, none of which would be solved by treating them as purely business clients.

Council. The newly founded group immediately conveyed a list of demands to the Housing Authority. As a pressure tactic, they organized a phone-in at their first meeting. Tenants were instructed to jam the Housing Authority switchboard by calling ten times a day, saying "I want to live in freedom" and then hanging up. Also at this meeting the organization's first chairman, Curtis Jones, was elected. He was later to become the main architect of the Rogers Point rent strike.

The Housing Authority continued to be conciliatory. O'Rourke felt that time and patience would be required for him to make amends for the policies and practices that he had inherited. As a further indication of his sincerity, O'Rourke immediately instituted several reforms. The much despised policy of charging tenants extra for paying their rents late was dropped. Most important, a temporary moratorium was called on all scheduled evictions. During this interim, the Housing Authority would meet with various tenant organizations to further identify and evaluate tenant problems.

The task of working on a day-to-day basis with various tenant representatives was delegated to Douglas Edwards, a black, who was appointed to the Housing Authority's second highest post, Assistant Executive Director. Beginning his job in early April 1966, about one month after the sit-in, Edwards sought and obtained a further extension on the eviction moratorium. He thought that moving on evictions just after arriving on the job would obstruct his chances of improving relations with tenants and those who claimed to be their spokesmen.

Edwards, however, was unable to develop a working relationship with the tenant community. He was able to accede to certain demands, but claimed that others which he supported in principle required more time, planning, and money. In South Peak, strong desire was expressed for a large-scale rehabilitation program, but the Housing Authority argued that it had no funds available for anything beyond normal maintenance. O'Rourke made a special trip to Washington to seek money for this purpose but was unsuccessful. On another important issue, the newly formed tenants' organization demanded that it be officially designated as the exclusive bargaining agent for the City's public housing tenants. The Housing Authority's position was to discuss grievances with any and all tenant groups, so on this issue as well as others, there was an impasse. Edwards developed a reputation in the community for being more pro-establishment than black. He and O'Rourke, on the other hand, were becoming increasingly discouraged over the prospects of reaching any accord with the more influential tenant leaders.

Meanwhile, the Housing Authority's non-eviction policy, rather than creating good will, was encouraging rent delinquency. Realizing that this policy was accumulating financial debts rather than moral credit, the agency wanted to begin evicting again. But fear of riot, which was probably of some concern throughout, now became stronger. With summer arriving, the agency believed that ghetto tensions were likely to be greater and more readily inflamed by any incident. They decided, therefore, to postpone evictions until the summer had passed.

Unfortunately for the Housing Authority, the anxieties over possible riot dominated its policies even after the summer. In early autumn, the City realized its worst fears. A full-scale riot erupted in South Peak. Two days later, just as the riot was being contained, Curtis Jones, president of the Presentation City Tenant Council, organized a demonstration at City Hall. He had threatened to appear with 200 pickets, but only twelve turned out. Despite the poor showing, he insisted that there would be more violence and bloodshed unless living conditions were improved in the City's public housing projects. The Housing Authority was taking no chances and extended the moratorium. No doubt, the political climate created by the South Peak riot was a major factor in sustaining the moratorium. Public officials and citizens alike expressed concern with how to improve the living conditions of the City's ghetto inhabitants. Evicting tenants in the aftermath of the riots would have been inappropriate and dangerous.

Furthermore, with the mayoralty election approaching, the mayor was moving cautiously. If he were to rescind the moratorium he would risk a political backlash from his liberal supporters and jeopardize his chances of winning. So his administration, which had tentatively adopted a non-eviction policy based upon a permissive, liberal ideology, was later forced to maintain it for reasons of political expediency. The decision was made to postpone evictions until after the elections. The long moratorium on evictions was a major factor that made it possible to sustain a rent strike for fourteen months in Rogers Point.

CHAPTER TWO

RACE POLITICS IN THE GRANADA POVERTY PROGRAM

WINNING neighborhood control of the poverty program was a major coup with far-reaching consequences. In each of the several poverty target areas of the City, poor residents elected delegates to their respective area boards, which were in turn empowered to establish policy for their community. With a majority of the delegates on the central Economic Opportunity Council elected by the neighborhoods, local programs were bound to be rubber stamped for approval. However, formal local autonomy did not necessarily mean that the organizers could altogether escape political pressures from the establishment. Public officials could intervene through the main office of the poverty program, or even more directly when necessary. In consultation with several pro-establishment black leaders, the mayor had appointed, before losing control of the poverty program, a young black stock broker as executive director of the downtown office. He was able to keep this position even after the mayor's defeat, and despite tremendous tensions between his office and some of the neighborhoods, no majority on the Economic Opportunity Council was of one mind to replace him.

In his dealings with the local poverty communities, he had the upper hand in several ways. The main office had considerable resources at its command with which to assist the neighborhoods with their programs. Also, his office was entrusted with responsibility for seeing that the local areas followed federal and city-wide regulations. Finally, though the local communities were autonomous politically, some of the poverty program bylaws were still vague enough to be interpreted in favor of downtown interests.

With these advantages, he soon became embroiled in a power struggle with some of the neighborhoods. His major aim was to recapture as much authority as he could for the main office. But he also wanted to assure a poverty program that would reflect, or at least not jeopardize, the best interests of the City, as defined by various office holders and agencies. Whether by withholding resources or absorbing the energy of local administrators in efforts to circumvent downtown decisions, he could make local administrators think twice before allowing their organizers to operate beyond permissible establishment limits. The political ambitions of many local administrators also gave the establishment access to the various local poverty target areas. Men eager to obtain city-wide political posts were likely to be sensitive to the interests of the establishment. Public officials could appeal to them directly if trouble was brewing, and often, when these administrators themselves could anticipate problems, even this step was not necessary.

Hector Lopez, the executive director of the Granada area of the poverty program where the Rogers Point rent strike occurred, was one of the local administrators who was somewhat vulnerable to political pressure. Hector * was a dedicated administrator who worked from early morning until late at night, Sundays not excepted, and he was quite serious about developing effective community pro-

---

* Those individuals with whom I was on a first-name basis, and also those I knew well, are generally referred to by their first names.

grams. Himself a Mexican, he was particularly committed to developing social and economic programs for the Spanish-speaking, who constituted approximately one-quarter of the residents in the Granada. Several difficult confrontations with the main office left him discouraged and enervated. He believed that maintaining good working relations with the downtown office was in the best interests of the Granada, and he had political ambitions of his own beyond the poverty program. As he told his friends, he wanted to obtain a city-wide political appointment. He was anxious to build a reputation as an effective and responsible administrator, which would make him eligible when vacancies opened or new positions were created. In short, Hector viewed his job with the poverty program both as a service to the community and as a stepping stone in his career.

Establishment officials affronted by organizers in the Granada therefore had a basis for pressuring Hector to intervene on their behalf. As the chief administrator of the target area, he had considerable formal powers over his staff: he could formally demand that they cease certain engagements, or at least burden them with other responsibilities which would make it extremely difficult for them to fulfill their political commitments. As a last resort he could recommend to the area board that they be fired.

Hector initially supported the efforts of the Rogers Point organizers in the rent strike. He was liberal politically, and sympathetic to their aims. He had no wish to incur the wrath of downtown officials, but he was not the kind of person to forsake a cause simply because pressure was being applied. As the strike progressed, however, he became increasingly critical of the organizers' political style. Agitating openly as poverty program organizers, they made militant public speeches, picketed City Hall, and in other ways called public attention to what they believed were the crimes of the establishment. Furthermore, as the strike continued, they did not appear to be reaching a settlement. Hector began to decide that the strike was not proving helpful to the cause of the tenants, and was becoming very embarrassing for the Granada poverty program.

But although Hector and other high-echelon administrators became progressively more disenchanted with the strike, they also became increasingly powerless to intervene. The organizers soon developed considerable political autonomy within the Granada, and were able to engage in virtually any controversial activity they chose without the effective intrusion of the poverty program administrators. The rent strike was among the major activities that they conducted on their own terms. What follows is a detailed account of how this state of affairs came about. It will become clear why, as organizers of the strike, they were able to enjoy the advantages of being associated with the poverty program while avoiding the attendant obligations and restraints, as defined by their superiors.

II

In the various political confrontations between the Mexican leadership of the Granada poverty program and the four black organizers in the Rogers Point district, two very different styles of political conduct became apparent: the blacks tended to adopt a non-negotiable political stance, while the Mexicans engaged essentially in a politics of compromise. Hector and other leaders continually attempted to develop a consensus with the black organizers. But the group from Rogers Point, who regarded their own political principles as unassailable, remained antagonistic to the Mexican administrators.

A no-compromise posture was regarded as appropriate by the organizers because they believed that their various demands were both justified and achievable. They were morally indignant and politically confident from almost the beginning of their employment with the poverty program. Two prior political events contributed toward shaping this style: the gains of the militant wing of the civil rights movement, and the passage of the Economic Opportunity Act, which created the poverty program.

The militant activists of the civil rights movement believed that direct action campaigns and disruptive strategies were much more likely to gain concessions from the power structure than pleading for assistance or developing allies. The massive picketing and sit-in activities at a prominent Presentation City hotel served as a prototype. These militants did not, basically, aim to reduce patronage by appealing to the sympathy of the public, but rather by inconveniencing actual and potential customers regardless of whether they were sympathetic. In this instance, they scored a major victory, despite claims by others that they were alienating the public. Such experiences convinced various leaders that the ability of blacks to win demands was directly related to their capacity to intimidate white institutions.

The enactment of the anti-poverty program was viewed by blacks and non-blacks alike as a major public concession to the militant civil rights movement. But the aim of the Economic Opportunity Act was construed, at least by blacks, as being primarily to reduce black poverty. Not only did passage of the act demonstrate to many of them the efficacy of militant politics, but it officially sanctioned their moral indignation—now even the federal government was recognizing both the injustice done to blacks and its responsibility to help them economically and socially.

The beneficiaries of the poverty program, however, were not only blacks. Other minority groups and whites as well had been sharing the limited resources made available through the Economic Opportunity Act. Believing that they had won the poverty program by their own efforts, black spokesmen in Presentation City stated on numerous occasions that the other poor should be thankful for what they had obtained for them. In political battles that crossed race lines, non-blacks were repeatedly reminded of this political debt. Widespread ethnic participation in the poverty program generated a mood of considerable indignation among black participants.

This mood had been further fueled by the successful battle against the mayor for control of the poverty program by the poor. Though broad support for neighborhood control of the program developed during the political battle, the black leadership unquestionably played the leading role. They were aggressive and uncompromising when other groups were both willing to settle for less than community control to avoid delays in the release of federal funds. For the blacks, this victory confirmed the efficacy of their militant stance and reinforced their conviction that other participants in the poverty program owed them a debt.

The events described thus far materially shaped the political expectations of blacks in Presentation City. It affirmed their right to make demands, and they also learned to expect concessions from others. What is more, these same events simultaneously influenced the perspectives of other minority groups and Caucasians. They, too, came to believe that improving the social and economic conditions of blacks deserved major priority, and that many blacks were quite prepared to wage a relentless, aggressive war, with no holds barred, in order to achieve their goals.

The respective interpretations of the political scene held by blacks and non-blacks generally influenced city politics, and more specifically, they played a major role in shaping the structure of control of the poverty program. On virtually all the local area boards, blacks were over-represented as delegates. In areas where blacks are the largest ethnic group, it has been extremely difficult for non-blacks to gain representation. For example, in the South Peak target area, where the Spanish-speaking represented 15 per cent of the poor, they occupied only one of twenty-five area board seats. In the Center Point target area, blacks controlled 25 per cent of the seats on the area board, even though they constituted only 10 per cent of the poor residents. Black demands, presented in a militant political style, were likely to be favored in political struggles.

Unlike the blacks in Presentation City, the Mexicans had not yet accrued political capital to draw upon. More recently, Mexican-Americans have been asserting themselves as a minority group, but in the early 1960's the lack of recognition that they constituted a minority whose problems deserved public attention was a favorite subject of conversation among Mexican leaders. By way of characterizing their situation, they would point out that they were classified as Caucasian by the Bureau of Census. No matter how complimentary they may have considered this, they believed that it entailed an enormous political cost.

The battle for control of the Granada poverty program provided an opportune occasion for them to assert their minority status. The Granada was initially organized and controlled by Caucasians, who also had the largest number of delegates on the area board. The executive director, too, was Caucasian. A four-month battle for control of the program ensued between the Mexicans and Caucasians. The small black minority was inactive then. The Mexican leader, Ramon Juarez, who led the fight to displace the white leadership, repeatedly asserted that the poverty program was for the benefit of minority groups who had special problems, as the Mexicans did, and that only they could develop programs that would reflect their own needs.

Ramon further argued that minority groups elsewhere

—namely, the Chinese and the blacks—controlled other target areas. The Mexicans deserved an opportunity to operate their own program. He cited the fact that the Mexicans and other Spanish-speaking citizens were concentrated in the Granada area. Further, Spanish-speaking citizens constituted one of every four of its residents. The Mexicans not only would be in a position to develop programs for their own ethnic group, but would represent the best interests of Spanish-speaking citizens in general.

Though the Mexican population was concentrated in the Granada, Ramon's argument was not altogether on solid ground. First, Mexicans in the Granada made up less than half of its Spanish-speaking citizens, and only slightly more than 10 per cent of the Granada population. Actually, their numbers in the community were approximately the same as blacks. Second, the Mexicans could not really speak for the more than twenty other Spanish-speaking ethnic groups in the Granada. Though sharing a common language, they were by no means a homogeneous grouping, and were often hostile toward each other. A Puerto Rican group, in fact, once sent a delegation to the downtown poverty office to protest that Mexicans were hoarding the jobs.

However, during the struggle for control of the Granada poverty program, there were no other Spanish-speaking factions competing for power. Ramon was able to convince the area board delegates that a Mexican was entitled to occupy the primary leadership role. The executive director was forced to resign, and was soon replaced by a Mexican. Later, eighteen Mexicans and five blacks were elected to the twenty-five-member Granada Area Board. Since both Mexicans and blacks were over-represented, it was largely at the expense of Caucasians and other Spanish-speaking groups. But the principle that the poverty program was presumably meant for ethnic minorities was, at least, tentatively established.

Though the Mexicans won a decisive victory, it was a precarious one. Later on they suffered serious reversals, which increased the number of black delegates to the area board in addition to electing several other non-Mexicans. Caucasians, on the whole, tended to stay away from the program. But neither blacks nor any other minority group accepted the view that the Mexicans in the Granada deserved a poverty program of their own.

The politically pluralistic character of the Granada made it impossible for the Mexicans to feel secure about their control of the program. They were always confronted with challenges by formidable citizens and organizations who viewed Mexicans primarily as a political threat and not as an ethnic group with special problems that somehow activated their consciences. These factors played a role in contributing to the air of reasonableness and the politics of compromise adopted by the Mexicans in the Granada. This political context also set the stage on which the rent strike organizers and the Mexican leaders clashed bitterly, a stage which formally began with the hiring of Curtis Jones, who led the rent strike in Rogers Point.

III

When Curtis Jones applied for a job as a community organizer, Hector suggested instead that he make out an application for the position of assistant director, the second highest administrative post. Hector was impressed with Curtis; he was articulate, had a commanding demeanor, was well educated, and could speak Spanish fluently. The fact that a Mexican executive director would be willing to consider hiring a black for a top post may seem unusual, since the Mexicans themselves wanted more patronage in the poverty program. Certainly, jobs were one major reason why various factions in the Granada, as well as in other target areas of the City, competed for control.

But Hector had good reasons to consider a black. First, the relatively tenuous political position of the Mexicans in the Granada favored a broad hiring policy at all levels, one which was not based exclusively on ethnic considerations. The Mexicans were repeatedly called upon to defend their hiring practices, which various citizens and groups complained were not really representative of the Granada. Those who had contact with the Mexican administrators soon learned how anxious they were to show the community that they were "fair-minded." In fact, the Mexicans were later able to boast of having the most integrated staff in the City's poverty program.

Second, Hector and many other Mexican leaders shared the same set of attitudes toward the problems of blacks as liberal Caucasians did. The political events described earlier created a climate of opinion in the City which influenced Mexicans as well as Caucasians. Hector believed that blacks were at the bottom rung and, though quite ambivalent, he did think that their situation deserved major priority and considered it reasonable that the poverty program should, to a large extent, be oriented toward them.

The Mexican community was caught in a peculiar trap. Hector, like most other Mexican leaders, was fairly well acculturated. On the one hand, he could hardly speak Spanish, which caused some of his opponents to mock him. This "handicap" represented and also created cleavages between himself and other Mexicans. Also, many of Hector's close friends and associates were Caucasians. Being acculturated meant losing a certain amount of Mexican identity, and it simultaneously placed Hector in a better position to understand the situation of other ethnic groups. It is not surprising, then, that he prided himself on being fair-minded. As an acculturated Mexican, his willingness to consider a black for a high post seemed to him quite natural and justifiable.

Curtis was not interested in the position of assistant director. He considered himself a radical and had serious doubts about being employed by the poverty program at all. In his mind, a top administrative post was a "fink" position tailored for those who did not object to "selling out." Hector hired him as a community organizer pending the approval of the Granada area board. When Curtis appeared before the board, the delegates questioned him in great detail about his background and experience, and in ways that reflected their inexperience as well as their involvement. They treated him no differently than other candidates in this sense, but Curtis believed that they were treating him offensively and walked out of the interview. This could have prompted the area board delegates not to hire him, or at least to assume that he was no longer interested. Instead, they reacted without indignation and approved him for the community organizer position. Curtis was notified and accepted the job.

Two months later, Hector promoted Curtis to the position of district supervisor of Rogers Point. Hector had not really thought about Curtis' behavior at the area board, although he later remarked that Curtis would be very difficult to get along with. But in any case, he was impressed with Curtis' leadership abilities. Curtis was assigned three organizers and provided with a separate district office and meeting room in the community. Though Rogers Point was racially integrated, its public housing project was virtually all black. In the expectation that these tenants would be the main recipients of services, all the organizers assigned to the district office were also black.

The Mexican coordinator of the Granada CAP, Arturo Martinez, who was directly responsible for the organizing activities of its five district offices, and would therefore be in regular contact with Curtis, argued with Hector about the promotion. According to Arturo, Curtis was politically militant and personally hostile. Hector did not agree. Their different opinions of Curtis reflected, generally, a different outlook on political issues. Politically, Arturo was regarded by others as conservative. He was extremely critical of any anti-establishment activities and had definite ideas about how subordinates should relate to their superiors. He believed that one's superiors should be unequivocally respected, and that those who failed to acknowledge this principle should be disciplined. He therefore reacted quite adversely to Curtis, who showed little deference, actual or symbolic, toward those to whom he was answerable. In tone, demeanor, and point of view, Curtis related to those in higher positions as if he were their equal or even their superior. Arturo interpreted this behavior as evidence of defiance and hostility.

Hector, who was much more representative of the Mexican leadership in the Granada, had a very different orientation. In fact, it would have been most unlikely for Hector to have hired Arturo, who had been employed with the Granada CAP before Hector was appointed. Being politically liberal, Hector was much more tolerant of militants. Though his own style was moderate, he believed that a militant stance was occasionally warranted. He saw the advances made by the civil rights movement and wanted Mexicans, like blacks, to assert themselves politically.

Hector's own willingness to openly challenge the establishment was indicated by his joining with numerous organizations and citizens of the community to publicly oppose a redevelopment plan. When he addressed himself to various officials at public meetings on the Redevelopment Agency's proposal, he effectively played the role of the angry community leader. In a public speech, he warned City Hall that the community would not tolerate any plan imposed upon it. But interestingly enough he seemed to share with many other Mexican-American leaders in the community— Arturo not included—a difficulty in conceiving of himself as a person vested with authority. Though he actually held an important position of authority, he seemed neither relaxed when giving orders nor really offended when his directives were violated. Not expecting any deference, he was much less likely than Arturo to be disturbed by or even to notice defiance and hostility. It was not surprising, then, that Hector promoted Curtis.

Curtis had a different interpretation of things. Many months later, I asked him why he was promoted. Curtis, who tended to be contemptuous of Mexican-Americans, explained that Hector's hand was really forced: he was compelled to fill this position with a black, and since Curtis had considerable experience, not to have promoted him would have created an embarrassing situation for the administrators. His response in this instance was revealing, because it indicated how he generally interpreted his gains. He assumed that virtually all gains or concessions from non-blacks were given grudgingly and had been obtained, directly or indirectly, by force. So whatever Curtis obtained, he saw no reason to feel thankful and could therefore not be expected to acknowledge any political debt, whether justified or not.

IV

Hector's commitment to improving conditions for the poor led to another major decision which had far-reaching implications for the political autonomy of the Rogers Point district office. It was a decision that Hector's allies interpreted as a reflection of his principles. To the organizers at Rogers Point, it was blatant opportunism. Hector urged the five district offices of the Granada to develop in their respective areas organizational structures independent of the poverty program. These organizations could move politically on local problems that concerned residents, such as welfare and slum housing. He was particularly interested in helping the Spanish-speaking community develop political muscle. He was convinced that by cultivating their own political resources poor residents would improve their bargaining position with the establishment. This route, he believed, would render the community less vulnerable to political pressure from public officials and influential citizens. Also, he wished to protect both the Granada poverty program and himself from adverse criticism and pressure. He believed that he could continue to exert influence over the character of these organizations because the organizers who would be putting these structures together were ultimately responsible to him.

On the whole, this strategy brought some desirable results. But the way in which the plan of action was interpreted and put into practice in the Rogers Point District made it operate somewhat differently from what Hector had intended. To the black organizers, Hector's suggestion was interpreted as a "cop out" and "sell out." They believed he was really saying that no political activity would be tolerated under the direct auspices of the poverty program. They were committed, on the other hand, to pushing the poverty program in a militant direction, and also wanted to be autonomous from the main office.

In order to meet this dual purpose, the organizers devised a strategy that accepted the principle of Hector's proposal. They set up a membership organization independent of the poverty program, which they called the Neighborhood Action Club (NAC). Curtis then appointed one of his organizers, Eddie Daniels, as chairman or nominal head of the organization. Though the organizers, incidentally, publicly claimed for NAC a membership of 400, it never actually exceeded two dozen, even though it nominally included all of the striking tenants. Even these two dozen were members in only the most limited sense, because NAC never became anything more than a political vehicle for these four organizers to operate autonomously. It was under the formal umbrella of this structure that the black organizers subsequently handled controversial issues.

The usefulness of setting up NAC was demonstrated many months after it was established, when the rent strike was being conducted. When the Mexican administrators criticized the way the organizers were handling the strike, they were told that they had no business intruding into the affairs of an independent organization. Simultaneously, the NAC organizers made it well known to others that they were organizers paid by the Granada EOC. They did not fret over this apparent inconsistency; they were serious about pressing the Granada poverty program to take radical public positions. The establishment could not bring direct pressure to bear on them as poverty program organizers; the structure of the poverty program necessarily required that they intervene through Hector, the executive director. But NAC was not afraid to deal with him. There were several reasons for this, as we will see, but certainly one of them was the political leverage they gained by setting up a formally independent organization.

NAC was only a front organization for the Rogers Point district office of the poverty program. The organizers operated during regular working hours and used the resources of the poverty program. All supplies, phone calls, and most important, the organizers' time were paid for by the poverty program. However, NAC was an unusual front organization. Rather than providing the district office with protection from other antagonistic agencies and officials, which would have served Hector's purpose of encouraging independent organizations, NAC used its independence to insulate itself from political pressures brought to bear upon it from within the Granada Community Action Program. Hector deeply regretted much later on that he had provided a vehicle by which these organizers could escape supervision. It was under the aegis of NAC that the rent strike was conducted, and he was unable to influence the course of the strike or other militant activities conducted by NAC. The black organizers felt they had scored a victory. They had beaten Hector at his own game and showed themselves to be more politically astute than he was.

V

Though creating a formal organizational apparatus independent of the poverty program rendered the black organizers relatively immune to direct criticism of their activities, they were not altogether invulnerable. They were accountable to the administrators for their use of facilities and how they spent their working hours. Hector and Arturo could have supervised their activities more closely and demanded that they devote more of their time to other projects. Tighter controls such as these would not have directly caused the organizers to end the strike, but they would have forced them to reevaluate their situation.

At the same time the strike began, the Granada held elections for delegates to the Granada Area Board. This event was significant because it did a great deal to further erode control over the organizers. Since the area board had ultimate control over the Granada poverty program, individuals or interest groups who wished to exert formal influence over its policies could run candidates. The basic requirements for becoming a delegate to the area Board were residence in the Granada and being poor.

Each district office was responsible for administering its own election. They were expected to leaflet the community and engage in any other activities that would encourage residents to vote. In each of the five districts that made up the Granada, residents would elect five delegates to the twenty-five-member board. The bylaws guiding these elections have varied from one year to another. In this particular election, candidates names did not have to be submitted beforehand to the Granada main office for a screening of eligibility. Whether they met the qualifications would be determined after elections.

The presumption was that more than five candidates would be running for election in each district in order to give voters a choice. However, since no list of nominations was submitted to the main office, there was no way of knowing how many candidates were actually running, how broadly representative they were, and whether they were qualified. This could readily invite election manipulation at the district office level. On election day, Arturo, the organizing coordinator, visited the district offices to watch the election proceedings. When he arrived late at Rogers Point, only the organizers were there. He learned that no one had voted yet. He remained at the office for about an hour, and still no resident appeared.

The following day, Curtis came to the main office to submit a list of delegates elected to the area Board. Arturo, who was furious, told Curtis that he refused to accept the candidates because he didn't believe that any residents had voted. Curtis insisted that Arturo was making an outrageous assertion, since he had been present for a only short time. Curtis could only conclude, therefore, that Arturo was a bigot. But Arturo remained adamant and informed Hector of his decision not to accept the election results at Rogers Point. He called for another election, but Hector overruled him. He told Arturo that he was taking things much too seriously, and unnecessarily stirring up trouble. To have supported Arturo, of course, would have meant engaging in a major political battle.

Those who had known Hector for some time were quite aware that he tended to avoid conflict whenever possible, regardless of his own point of view. This is why many considered him passive. Ramon, the Mexican leader who successfully convinced the area board to unseat the "anglo" executive director, was disappointed with Hector's inability to push hard. Ramon, who was well acquainted with Hector, originally proposed him for the position of executive director. He knew that Hector was not assertive, but when scouting around for other potential Mexican applicants, he found that they generally suffered the same limitation. As already mentioned, many of the Mexican-American leaders in the community were generally ill at ease in positions of authority. Hector, on the other hand, did have certain skills, including an ability to speak effectively in public, and Ramon thought that with experience he would eventually be able to handle the demands of the job effectively.

Hector's decision to overrule Arturo, however, did not head off conflict. Curtis and his organizers were not appeased. Still affronted by what they considered a racist act, they attended the next area board meeting to protest. They demanded, unsuccessfully, that Arturo be fired. Arturo would also have preferred to dismiss Curtis. But even if Hector had agreed in principle, the politics of the poverty program would have made it extremely difficult for a non-black to fire a black. Charges of racism would have generated protests and mobilized opposition. In short, neither the Mexicans nor the blacks could rid themselves of each other, and it was within this context that the political struggles between them ensued.

This area board meeting was the first in a series of what appeared to be humiliation rituals, in which the organizers would put down the Mexican leadership as well as the area Board delegates themselves. Even though most of the Mexican delegates, who constituted eighteen of the twenty-five members on the Board, were unable to understand or speak English, the meetings were always conducted in English, and one Mexican would briefly translate the proceedings. However, when the black organizers crashed these meetings —they never asked for permission to attend—there was neither sufficient time nor the appropriate atmosphere in which to translate what occurred. With much gusto, they made rapid-fire charges and denunciations of the program's administrators. The Mexican delegates, more often than not, failed to grasp what NAC was complaining about, and NAC, in turn, did not really care.

The election incident appreciably undermined the authority of the administrators. Hector, by overruling Arturo, flouted regulations that he was entrusted to enforce. Election rules were an important component of the program's bylaws, and Hector's unwillingness to insist that they be followed gave the organizers virtual license to violate other rules. Further, the authority of Curtis' immediate superior, Arturo, was considerably undermined. Arturo understood that in dealing with these organizers in the future he could not always count on Hector to support his decisions. Curtis and the other organizers learned that whenever they had serious differences with Arturo, they could simply bypass him and appeal to Hector. There was no longer even a practical reason to respect Arturo. At meetings of the full Granada organizing staff, NAC would openly demean him, calling his proposals "Mickey Mouse" and irrelevant or harmful to the interests of the poor. Arturo became little more than a figurehead.

Hector, who had undercut his own authority, further undermined it by permitting the organizers to make protests directly to the area board. He never complained to them that they were circumventing him. In the election incident, Hector had made a decision favorable to the organizers; they were therefore not attending the board meeting to reverse an unfavorable act. But the idea of establishing rules to specify under what conditions staff could appeal to the area board never seemed to occur to him. Perhaps the political atmosphere was such that a tighter control structure would have seemed inconsistent with the maximum feasible participation conception of the poverty program. But the danger was clear; Hector too might be reduced to a figurehead.

This election established a precedent. It made the NAC organizers even more daring when a special election was held several months later to replace delegates who had resigned from the area board. In accordance with changes in the bylaws, they submitted a list of nominees to the main office, but they refused to say when the election would be held. The main office was not responsible for setting the date for such elections. Arturo nevertheless insisted that the district office inform him of the election date so that he could visit their office then. The organizers had not forgotten the last incident with Arturo. Curtis again accused him of racism, and said, "Blacks are not children. They can supervise their own elections." They secretly elected delegates, this time without any repercussions from the main office in the Granada.

The organizers interpreted these victories as a product of their aggressive, uncompromising stance. They also believed that the Mexicans were easy to intimidate. In fact, George Franklyn, one of the black organizers, claimed that "Mexicans are all cowards." They did not consider alternative explanations, that Hector's political response was not simply a cowardly response to their aggressiveness. Personally, Hector tended to be a compliant person, and he believed that a leader should make every effort to get along with his staff, because unity, rather than divisiveness, was required to build a strong organization. Accordingly, Hector routinely acceded to requests by other staff members who were not aggressive, though what they wanted to do sometimes ran against his own views.

Hector's style was often beneficial to the functioning of the Granada poverty program. He got along extremely well with the Mexican staff members, who respected his willingness to give them a great deal of latitude. In turn, he had no difficulty enlisting their support when he needed it. He did not realize soon enough that his permissiveness toward the conduct of the blacks, even when in violation of stated regulation, would not be reciprocated and would only reinforce their political recalcitrance. This was a wholly new experience for him.

The black organizers were not trading favors with the Mexicans. They viewed their victories as hard-earned and not gratuitously attained. Of course, the method of judgment implied in their aggressive stance made it almost impossible for them to detect concessions voluntarily given. To illustrate, on one occasion they threatened to beat Hector physically in order to force him to give in on an issue. Hector certainly didn't like being threatened, but he reacted to the situation with humor, and granted their request because he did not see it as being of major importance. However, the organizers could only assume that a direct causal relationship existed between their attempt to intimidate him and his willingness to bow to their demand.

Returning to the election issue, one might suppose that the organizers subverted the election procedures to assure that the elected delegates would represent their interests. But, in reality, there was no opposition then in the community. Of course, one never knows what risks might be entailed when holding open elections. This consideration probably deterred them from taking chances. Yet later on, when one candidate opposed to the policies of these organizers ran for election, he was easily defeated by NAC.

Their resistance to having open elections was largely a reaction to the mandate from the Granada main office. They considered it humiliating to take any orders from the Mexicans. They believed that the maximum feasible participation concept should apply fully to their own operation, and this meant to them nothing less than complete autonomy. They proceeded to behave as if they were independent. They continually violated official regulations and challenged the right of Mexican administrators to make any demands, however mild. In manipulating the elections, then, the organizers were more concerned with expressing their independence than with consolidating their political power on the area board.

Had Hector successfully challenged the organizers' usurpation of the election process, they still would have elected their own supporters in another election, but the bylaws established by the area board would have remained intact. In defending his refusal to invalidate the election results, Hector had told Arturo that another election would not have made any practical difference. He was probably right in this case, but he overlooked the long-range consequences for his program. By failing to assert his authority in the crucial area of electing delegates, he weakened the control structure of the Granada EOC, most particularly with regard to its relationship to the program in the Rogers Point district.

The election incident was only one in a series of acts

that shaped the respective expectations of the Mexicans and the black organizers. Hector himself would be likely to feel increasingly awkward asserting authority, since he tended to encourage its violation. Also, the organizers would react more indignantly and strongly to any belated attempts by Hector to assert himself. In other words, Hector's permissive response to the various demands of the organizers fed and further consolidated their expectations that the Rogers Point district was, after all, an autonomous operation. By the time Hector became sharply critical of the conduct of the rent strike, he was in a poor position to influence their behavior.

VI

To those who were most familiar with the politics of the Granada, there was good reason to believe that in the long run the Mexican community would dominate the local poverty program. By controlling the area board they would presumably control the program. Further, the area board seemed to be the one structure that had initially shown promise of being able to control the black organizers. Eighteen of twenty-five delegates were Mexicans, and behind them stood a highly experienced Mexican leader in the City, Juan Ramirez. Through his diligence and political resources, he was responsible for the election of a predominantly Mexican board. It was presumed by many familiar with the local political scene that he would provide the program with guidance, and that by controlling the largest block of votes on the area board, he would be in a position to assure Mexican leadership of the Granada poverty program.

Ramirez had gained considerable political power as president of a social-political organization called the Amigos. He was a business agent of the Laborers Union (AFL-

CIO), which was one-third Mexican and whose members were deeply devoted to him. He organized the Amigos mainly in order to maintain a Mexican power base in the union. As president of the organization and business agent for the union, he was in a reasonably good position to represent Mexican interests. Ramirez wanted to use his political base to extend his control into the Granada community. He viewed the poverty program as an excellent organizational vehicle for achieving his aim. By getting the Amigos out to vote en masse, he was responsible for the election of a substantial majority of delegates to the area board. He was therefore in an ideal position to exert effective control over the Granada poverty program.

However, formal Amigos' control of the program did not turn out to be actual political control. To have effectively wielded power, the Amigos delegates would have needed Ramirez' active involvement in the politics of the program. They were simply unable to provide leadership on their own. All of them were poor, politically inexperienced, and very ill at ease at area board meetings. We have already noted that only a few of them actually understood English, though the meetings were conducted in that language. According to the secretary of the area board, who was also Mexican, these delegates frequently voted on issues without realizing what they were voting for. At least some of them tended to be too self-conscious to inquire further. There were usually a considerable number of visitors to the area board meetings, and this undoubtedly heightened their self-consciousness.

Ramirez was unable to become involved in the political affairs of the poverty program because of the demands of his union activities. Being regularly involved in the poverty program would have required that he overextend himself, which he had not anticipated. A second deterrent to his involvement was his distaste for being considered by others the "boss" of a political machine. He found the image disturbing, even though he played the role. For example, when attending one meeting at the area board, he had overheard a disparaging remark about his political machinations. According to one of his close associates, this kind of criticism kept him from attending any other meetings.

A concern for his image was also related to his city-wide political interests. He was appointed to the Human Rights Commission, and in general he enjoyed being politically involved at the city-wide level. Later on, his organization, Amigos, devoted its energies to getting out the vote in a mayoralty contest. As Presentation City had a reputation among its citizens of having a clean government, he felt uncomfortable with his own reputation as a political boss. This further discouraged him from participating in the political affairs of the poverty program.

However, there was one unusual exception. Sometime after the area board elections, the chairman of the area board stated that one of the black delegates from Rogers Point could not be seated. He had learned that the delegate was an employee of the poverty program, which, according to the bylaws, represented a conflict of interest. This immediately touched off a row in which the Mexicans were accused of being racists. A Mexican delegate was manhandled, and several were threatened. One black, in fact, displayed a weapon. Meanwhile, someone phoned Ramirez, who swiftly sent to the meeting about twenty armed Amigos. They took seats in the audience, and were ready to intervene if more trouble occurred. Apparently they neutralized the situation, but the meeting, which was too tense to continue, disbanded.

There were no further attempts to unseat the black delegate. The Amigos seemed satisfied with proving that they were not to be intimidated. Even Ramirez had no interest in following through on this matter. The chairman had been simply following the bylaws, and with the combined assistance of the Amigos and the central downtown office, he could have made the regulation stick and unseated the delegate. But to have done so, would have meant becoming embroiled in even more conflict, which the Mexican delegates clearly did not want. Unlike the blacks in the Granada, who liked a good fight, these Mexicans preferred to avoid trouble.

It is ironic that the one significant occasion upon which the area board delegates acted affirmatively and in concert was the reinstatement of Curtis, who had been fired by a new executive director. Hector, weary of poverty program politics, finally resigned, but just before doing so he became acquainted with a fairly new arrival in the City, John La-Salle. Impressed with LaSalle's aggressive style, which he had come to believe was more appropriate than his own for the top administrative post, Hector recommended to the area board delegates that they hire LaSalle as a replacement. LaSalle was presumably half-Mexican, though others claimed later that he was not really Mexican at all; in any case, his style was markedly different from that of other community leaders in the Granada. Not wanting to repeat what he considered the mistakes of his predecessor, he attempted to establish his authority over the Granada program by ruling with a firm hand. As soon as he was hired, he began ordering about staff members in a manner that they regarded as disrespectful. Some had friends on the area board to whom they complained about his behavior.

A major organizational explosion was set off when he hired, with the area board's approval, an organizing coordinator to replace Arturo, who had also resigned. This new staff member, who had formerly resided in the Granada, lived elsewhere when he was hired. To the staff in the Granada, employing persons who lived beyond the Granada boundaries was taboo. The organizers and other staff members protested. Curtis, along with another district supervisor, issued a press release criticizing John LaSalle's action. He responded by firing both of them. But Carmen Perez, the Mexican supervisor who was dismissed, had considerable political leverage in the Granada, and was able to force him to rescind his decision. However, he refused to rehire Curtis.

Meanwhile, the area board was furious that he had fired staff members without their sanction; the bylaws stated that employees could only be fired with the approval of the area board. The issue soon became a power struggle between the new director and the area board. In addition, protests were growing over what was designated as the racially discriminatory act of firing Curtis. The fact that John LaSalle rehired the Mexican he had dismissed added fuel to the accusation of racial bigotry. The area board decided to overrule him and returned Curtis to his former position.

This final decision rendered Curtis and the other Rogers Point organizers virtually impervious to the control or influence of the Mexican administrators. A most important fact was established, one which the organizers had formerly suspected but which was now confirmed: they could not so readily lose their jobs. They had successfully shattered the formal control structure of the program, at least with regard to its implications for themselves, with the inadvertent assistance of the Mexican members.

VII

NAC's effectiveness came in part from its ability to maintain a remarkable degree of unanimity. Curtis Jones was considerably more committed ideologically than the other organizers, and on several issues they had important differences between themselves. But their mutual commitment to black unity was the paramount consideration when relating to the non-black community. This unity was reinforced by their tendency to interpret tensions that developed between themselves and the Mexicans as related essentially to the racist attitudes of the Mexicans.

There were many other occasions that seemed to them to justify this interpretation. For example, the organizers often requested the main Granada office to type and mimeograph letters or leaflets pertaining to the rent strike. Since office staff workers filled requests in the order that they were submitted, Rogers Point, along with the other district offices, had to wait its turn. This often took longer than they liked, and became the cause of many heated arguments. They believed that the main office would have been most willing to bypass regulations had it been Mexicans rather than blacks who were striking.

One incident that contributed considerably to their conviction that they were engaged in a race war with the Mexicans was Hector's attempt to transfer the Rogers Point operation to another target area. Hector's job, which he found difficult enough, was made even more taxing by the Rogers Point organizers. He was becoming increasingly tired and tense. When a new poverty target area, Center Point, was being formed, changes in the boundaries were being considered by the various target areas. Hector suggested to the South Peak EOC administrators that they annex Rogers Point. They accepted, pending downtown approval. Meanwhile, Hector informed Curtis and the other organizers of his proposal. They rejected it and indicated that they would not tolerate being transferred. They charged Hector with racism, claiming that he deliberately wanted to exclude blacks from participation in the Granada community. Under pressure from the organizers, Hector dropped the plan.

The many confrontations with the Mexicans, and in other settings with Caucasians, brought the organizers closer together. The various political positions they united around were shaped by Curtis' ability to link his own political and social perspectives to the mandate for black unity. As their formal supervisor, he was ideally situated to influence their attitudes and behavior. Curtis was able to use his leadership position to build loyalties, and he succeeded in creating an atmosphere at his office that tended to make their jobs more enjoyable and relaxing than they might have been. He was older and more experienced, and as a leader he was somewhat charismatic. Moreover, Curtis projected himself as an extremely self-sacrificing person.

The organizers respected Curtis a great deal and were anxious to support him whenever they could, just as he had regularly supported them as their supervisor. Under these circumstances, it was almost inevitable that insofar as black unity shaped the character of NAC, it would be shaped around the social and political policies of Curtis Jones. With regard to the rent strike, they were publicly one voice. And that voice, which was loud, angry, and defiant, could not be restrained or muffled by the other members of the poverty program, local or city-wide.

CHAPTER THREE

NAC AND
THE TENANTS

THOUGH Curtis Jones, the leader of the Neighborhood Action Club (NAC), came to the poverty program with a reputation as an experienced organizer of the poor, he could best be described as having been a leader without a following. Several months before being employed by the Granada target area, he and other minority leaders had organized the city-wide Presentation City Tenants Council (PCTC). The organization was conceived as a federation of local public housing tenant unions. Curtis became its first president, and under his leadership, its activities revolved largely around making public demands of the Housing Authority through picketing, leafleting, and issuing press releases. Usually, these activities were accompanied by threats of massive action, such as city-wide rent strikes and sit-ins.

Though the organization's occasional dramatic moments gave it a great deal of publicity, it was little more than a political umbrella for a congerie of leaders without a following. They spoke a great deal about developing a large membership base, but little or no effort was actually made to organize tenants around housing issues. Moreover, PCTC was unresponsive to outside assistance. The organization was unreceptive to support from the white community, though many of its members were concerned about public housing problems. Curtis, who prided himself on being a black power advocate, generally made no political distinctions between members of the establishment and other white citizens in Presentation City. Whites were generally treated antagonistically by Curtis and the organization; they were often threatened and given ominous warnings of things to come. Since PCTC neither built a base nor developed allies, its militance had limited potential, and it was unable to force the Housing Authority to accept its demands to improve conditions.

Curtis resigned as president of PCTC, but he still retained control over its policies. So, as the leader of the Rogers Point rent strike, he had access to a base, however fragile, beyond the community in which he worked. When he planned to picket or visit the mayor's office to complain about conditions in public housing, he was in a position to obtain a few supporters. Curtis considered his link to PCTC a useful political tool in agitating for better conditions in Rogers Point.

Though Curtis was both founder and leader of a militant tenants' organization, he had no experience with rent strike activities before coming to Rogers Point. The same was true of the other three members of NAC. With the exception of George Franklyn, none of them even lived in public housing. But in their contact with tenants as poverty program organizers, complaints against the Housing Authority were frequently vented, and they learned to act as advocates of individual tenants by conveying their respective complaints to the Housing Authority. Though they performed this task with gusto and sincerity, they generally agreed that it had limited utility. They began to consider collective action.

Curtis spoke to the other organizers about the advantages of a rent strike. Under his militant leadership, they had already tasted success in their battle against the Granada

EOC; why not take on the Housing Authority! The organizers realized that the Housing Authority's moratorium on evictions gave them a decided advantage. NAC then drew up a list of demands which they personally presented to John O'Rourke, the executive director of the Housing Authority.

At this meeting, O'Rourke was told by the NAC organizers that they considered their demands quite reasonable and were therefore expecting him to indicate immediately his intention of acting favorably upon them. O'Rourke insisted that he was in no position to act upon their demands right away. He was warned that the tenants had endured great hardships and that there was no more time left for hedging. Since they had apparently reached an impasse, NAC abruptly ended the meeting. Though nothing was settled, Curtis considered the meeting successful. His organizers emerged from the meeting angrier men, savoring a taste of victory after telling off a public official. They were convinced that O'Rourke was insincere and uninterested in poor tenants; by issuing an ultimatum to him and generally displaying disrespect, the organizers believed they had been successful in "putting him in his place." There is no doubt that their confrontation with O'Rourke brought them closer to striking.

Though the organizers were now psychologically prepared for a strike, no strike plans were made. They did not speak to any of the tenants about it, and did no planning among themselves. Meanwhile, leaders of another tenant union in the South Peak section of the City were publicly threatening a rent strike. Apparently, the organizers were waiting for them to move first; there were advantages in numbers. When Curtis learned that they had finally decided to strike, NAC immediately followed suit. Curtis gave the order and the other three organizers moved swiftly to contact tenants they already knew. They reminded tenants that the Housing Authority was not evicting anyone, and that "there are rent strikes all over the city now." They were able to recruit eighteen strikers, virtually all of them mothers on welfare.

In my many discussions with these tenants, I learned that they faced their situation with a combination of fear and apathy. Most of the striking tenants were paying rents of about $60 per month, which was substantially less than rents for similar apartments in the private market. Eviction from public housing, which was being risked by nonpayment of rents, could be financially disastrous to these poor families. They were understandably fearful of doing anything that could cause them to be evicted. On the other hand, they were unconvinced that housing conditions could be improved in Rogers Point even through pressure tactics. They generally considered the situation in public housing a hopeless mess, and apathetically fell into a grim acceptance of their life situation.

If apathy and fear essentially described the mood of the striking tenants, why were they willing to strike? First, their fears of reprisal for striking were substantially reduced by the well-known moratorium on evictions. The organizers continually reminded them that no evictions had taken place in almost six months, and that no more would occur. Second, the hostility of the tenants toward the Housing Authority was initially great enough to overcome even fear and apathy. The central role of hostility in sparking the strike deserves further comment.

A major source of tenant discontent was the deteriorated condition of public housing in Rogers Point and the unfair treatment that tenants believed they were accorded. As I have said, complaints about long delays and even failure to repair and maintain premises were widely voiced. Tenants were also troubled about Housing Authority practices which they considered unfair. As the Housing Authority itself acknowledged, those who had formerly administered the agency were, in fact, uninterested in the welfare of its tenants. If tenants occasionally suspected the agency of misdeeds for which, in truth, the current administrators were not responsible, this was understandable. But there was much more than trouble with the Housing Authority behind their anger and hostility. They were also frustrated in their encounters with schools, police, welfare agencies, and other institutions. They could certainly distinguish the practices of one agency from another, but at another level these distinctions occasionally seemed to break down. That is, they often appeared to react to a specific dilemma created by contact with one institution with the pent-up frustration and anger created by their contact with others. In a typical example of this, a lawyer gathering legal material on behalf of a striking tenant inquired about her grievances. She angrily reported waiting unnecessarily long for the Housing Authority to repair a toilet stoppage. In the interest of gathering precise information, the lawyer asked how long she had actually waited. She cried, "two hours." It seemed as if her total life situation, not just her encounters with the Housing Authority, had generated a low frustration tolerance. These accumulated tensions were among the reasons that tenants were willing to go on strike.

On the other hand, I found no evidence that tenants were actually hopeful of bringing about material changes in conditions. In my talks with them, they repeatedly expressed despair about improving things. One tenant, in explaining why she decided to strike, aptly captured the mood of the others by saying, " 'Cause I'm gonna shit on *them,* and see if *they* like it." Not hope for change, but accumulated anger and tension accounted for their willingness to strike.

II

The way in which the organizers related to these feelings of fear and apathy did much to shape their organizing strategy. Soon after the strike began, their initial outbursts of anger subsided. The tenants became anxious again about eviction and asked whether their strike could accomplish anything worthwhile; many tenants even balked at remaining on strike only a few weeks after its inception. Yet despite enormous resistance NAC successfully prevented any defections. None of the original strikers withdrew their money to return it to the Housing Authority. As we shall see, the organizers achieved success by using strategies that alienated tenants rather than involving them in the organization. This state of affairs, in turn, was influenced by three major factors: how NAC organized its resources to maintain contact with strikers; the characteristics of the tenants themselves; and how the tenants related to each other.

NAC made two important decisions about allocating its manpower on behalf of the strike. First, the task of dealing with the tenants was delegated exclusively to one organizer rather than to several of them. Second, this assignment was given to Jerry Cook, whose personal characteristics and position in NAC shaped his role as tenant organizer. Assigning only one organizer to relate to the tenants, no matter which one, was likely to impose upon him two major pressures: time and responsibility. Each one of the NAC organizers was a full-time employee who performed many tasks not related to rent strike activities, and these normally occupied a considerable part of the day. They had to attend many meetings, organize and participate in youth and adult recreation projects, and were involved in various issues, such as attempting to get free lunch programs started for poor public school students. Because cultivating tenants was also time-consuming, the organizer chosen for this task would be compelled to operate on a tight schedule; he would be responsible both for recruiting additional tenants and for making sure that strikers would not defect.

Second, the responsibility for blocking the flow of rent money from tenants to the Housing Authority placed enormous pressure and responsibility on one organizer. The strike, of course, could not be carried on without tenants withholding rent. Both of these factors, responsibility and limited time, discouraged any strategic diversions from the main task of seeing that the tenants remained on strike and continued to pay NAC their rent. For example, efforts to entice an ever larger number of tenants to join the strike, and to involve those already on strike more actively, would have been quite time-consuming. Even an organizer eager to try would be discouraged by the other pressures of his job.

If assigning just one organizer to the tenants reduced the chances of actively involving them, then selecting Jerry Cook virtually eliminated such opportunities. For one thing, his life style had not prepared him to be straightforward. Even in his role as organizer, he carried on brief, stormy, sexual affairs with tenants, borrowed money which was not always returned, and otherwise tended to manipulate these women. Whatever merits there were to bringing the strikers together at a meeting, Jerry would have been most embarrassed by such a confrontation. Also, he was too personally disorganized to develop on his own a concerted program of action for the tenants.

Further, if the way in which NAC related to the tenants reflected Jerry's relationship to them, it also reflected how NAC related to Jerry. Curtis "called the shots," and Jerry, along with the other organizers, was seldom actively involved in making decisions. Unlike the others, he was often not even notified about the progress of the strike. Several meetings were held with the Housing Authority and representatives from other agencies that he never learned about. There was no plan to withhold information from him, but often nobody bothered to inform him. Unless he pressed the other organizers for information, which he didn't, he was in no position to keep the tenants well informed. Jerry was not guided by Curtis in his conduct toward the tenants. His task was to see that the tenants remained on strike, and as long as he did that no questions were asked.

In short, NAC excluded the tenants from any activity other than withholding rent. Tenants were also cut off from information about the strike and would often receive distorted reports. Jerry's personal style favored exaggerations and inaccuracies, but his style of relatedness was also structurally encouraged. Since the tenants had little or no access to information about the strike, he was in a position to withhold, exaggerate, and distort, whichever would serve the interests of NAC.

Why was only one organizer assigned to the tenants, and why was it Jerry? Jerry was generally viewed as occupying a much lower status than the other members of the group. On the one hand, he was well liked by the others; Curtis recognized his "gift of gab," and this was one reason he was assigned to work with the tenants. However, Jerry looked and sounded like a "hood" according to NAC members. He was usually unshaven and dressed sloppily. He spoke loudly, rapidly, and gutturally. He also had a long police record. Jerry was anxious "to go straight" and he viewed his job as organizer with considerable pride. But none of the organizers believed that he was really seeking to change the quality of his life or, in their terms, "to better himself." He kept his old habits, such as drinking in a parked automobile after midnight and roving from one sexual affair to another. To the organizers, he was the type of poor black in the community that they wanted to help.

Curtis was well educated. He spoke several languages,

and although he had no college degree he had attended several colleges. Eddie Daniels, who tended to imitate Curtis, enjoyed advocating the value of education for black people. He was attending high school part-time and would occasionally boast about such scholastic feats as passing a mathematics course. George Franklyn, the only member of NAC who was a public housing tenant, had a wife and ten children and had been hoping to improve his family's situation for many years. He looked forward to moving out of public housing someday. George had entered college but had dropped out to support his family. He still occasionally worked as a musician on weekends to supplement his income. Jerry's very different style of life affected the way in which the other organizers viewed him.

The status distinctions perceived by Jerry and the others had important consequences for the conduct of the strike. It largely accounted for Jerry's assignment to the tenants. An excellent illustration of how status factors generally influenced choice of roles was revealed by an observation that Jerry himself made. Occasionally, Jerry would shoot crap in the evening with some of the men in order to gain their confidence. NAC was anxious to develop programs for the unemployed men in the area. George, who lived in the project, would never join these games. When asked why, Jerry explained, without resentment, that George was "like on a higher level" than him. For George to have participated in such games with these men would have undermined his leadership position. Jerry further explained that while he acted as their friend, George's role would be to provide guidance.

Apparently, it was not that tasks requiring frequent contact with the community were necessarily of low status. In the example cited above, relative status reflected just how these organizers related to the community. George's role as adviser to unemployed men was more prestigious than Jerry's role as friend. However, contact with community residents, as opposed to dealing with various groups outside the community, such as public agencies, had lower status, and was therefore less rewarding. For example, Jerry liked his work but he often felt that his efforts were not appreciated. Rewards tend to be commensurate with the evaluation of different tasks, and speaking to public housing tenants was not as highly esteemed as addressing public officials.

Interestingly, the organizers considered their respective roles as natural or given. Curtis, the oldest and most experienced, was the "brains" behind the operation. George, who was believed to be an eloquent speaker, generally addressed public officials at various meetings. Eddie, who was shy, was assumed to be an excellent writer. He wrote all the leaflets and handled correspondence to public officials. And, finally, Jerry was believed to "have a way" with the tenants.

Though there was some justification for the respective roles assigned to NAC organizers, there was little that was really natural about them. For example, Eddie in fact wrote very poorly. George was more confident in public but not really eloquent. On the other hand, he could have been considered "natural" for Jerry's post. Since he had been living in the projects for almost a decade, he had more contacts with tenants than Jerry. He was also a family man, stable, and, unlike Jerry, would not have been as prone to jeopardize the interests of the strike with a series of sexual affairs.

Jerry, on the other hand, could have been groomed to play a public role. With practice, he could have improved his speaking potential and developed a demeanor more appropriate for appearing in public. This is no unfounded conjecture. For another research project I needed a black male to present himself to various retail establishments downtown. When I told the organizers about my project, George volunteered. I selected Jerry, however, because I wanted to test the reaction of downtown proprietors to a more stereotyped low-income black. To my disappointment, Jerry appeared the next day clean-shaven and well dressed, and he presented himself to the downtown shopkeepers with considerable decorum. He spoke slowly and respectfully. I had given him no instructions, since I had assumed that he would behave "naturally." Jerry virtually destroyed the experiment and profoundly altered my image of him as a lower-class black who was frozen in his status.

Yet it was this view of Jerry that largely accounted for his being assigned to the tenant detail and determined how the other organizers related to him. It is not that these status distinctions between the organizers and Jerry made them behave toward him in a snobbish manner. They simply didn't think he would understand and appreciate the events that took place between themselves and persons beyond the borders of Rogers Point. From their point of view, there was just no reason to keep him informed.

The failure of the organizers to communicate with Jerry also reflected their views of the tenants. Because tenants were considered a relatively low status group, the organizers preferred to relate to other members of the Presentation City community. They shared some of the views of welfare mothers prevalent among white middle-class citizens. They believed that society was grossly side-stepping its responsibilities to these women, but they regarded them as unable to handle their own affairs and very unsophisticated, as George remarked, "in the ways of the world." George believed they could "make a dollar stretch" much further than white women in financial difficulties, but the organizers also believed that their background and lack of experience poorly equipped them to rise above their situation.

Defining these women as lower status persons served another purpose. All the organizers had generally occupied low status, poor-paying jobs when working at all. As men who often needed to boost their self-esteem, they appeared to have a stake in regarding these women as occupying a much lower rank than themselves. Throughout the strike, the organizers remarked how self-sacrificing they were on behalf of these welfare recipients. They repeatedly stressed that without their involvement in social action, the interests of these tenants would be abandoned. Without exception, each of them had, on several occasions, stated or implied that the women in Rogers Point would be unable to get along without them. To have attributed a higher status and permitted a more extensive role to these women during the strike would have been tantamount to raising doubts about their own competence. Just as mere suggestions from "outsiders" were considered an affront to Curtis, encouraging the participation of these women, or acknowledging their abilities to contribute favorably to the outcome of the strike, would have been an admission that they were unable to cope with the problems of the strike on their own.

This sensitivity, vulnerability, and readiness to interpret events as threats to self-esteem was considerable enough to be conspicuous. Though all four shared this tendency, Curtis exhibited it most strongly. And as their formal leader and one who possessed a great deal of influence over the others, his own patterns of relating tended to define those of the group. Whether around issues of self-esteem, attitudes toward the women strikers, or anything else, it was almost inevitable that the character and intensity of his outlook would affect the other organizers. Eddie, in fact, often imitated Curtis. Even his demeanor and speech habits gradually came to resemble those of Curtis. I soon realized that asking Eddie about his views became a useful way of determining what Curtis, who was more reticent, had in mind. It was not that Curtis created needs and values for them. But under his leadership he was often able to activate and exaggerate those that the organizers already possessed.

Still, the organizers might have kept the tenants informed about current developments. Unfortunately, the progress of the strike was not really satisfactory, and NAC really had nothing to boast about. Even if receiving pessimistic reports would not have encouraged tenant withdrawal from the rent strike, it might have generated demands that tenants be involved in planning strategies. So for organizational as well as for personal reasons, the organizers were committed to excluding tenants from participation.

Since NAC did not conduct tenant meetings, the tenants lacked an opportunity to collectively exchange views as to the leadership or to establish regular contact with each other. They were cut off from direct and indirect sources of information and excluded from participation. It was interesting, for example, that none of the strikers I spoke with actually knew how many tenants were on strike. This was amazing to me, but not to Jerry, who was able to operate on the assumption that any tactical ruse he employed would not be discovered.

Jerry's assumption would have been unwarranted if the strikers had been on friendly terms among themselves independent of their relations to NAC. But this was not the case. Many strikers reported having no friends in the projects, and most had no more than one or two. As an illustration of how isolated the strikers were, most of them did not even know whether other tenants in their buildings were on strike. Significantly, these tenants were generally unaware of the Housing Authority's most unusual practice, a vestige from the preceding administration, of charging higher rents for tenants on welfare than for those not on welfare but receiving the same income. To some extent, tenant isolation can be broken down through developing social and recreational facilities. Several projects offered these opportunities, but there were no such common gathering places for tenants in Rogers Point. The isolation of tenants from each other in this project reinforced the patterns established by NAC.

The characteristics of the tenants together with their life situation also contributed to their isolation. Their attitude toward other tenants whom they repeatedly spoke of disdainfully, reflected in part their own low self-esteem. Lack of self-respect could have readily bred social distance and hostility towards others similarly situated. Also, these tenants generally appeared tired; poor living conditions, little money, and large families imposed considerable hardships and tended to enervate them. Lack of energy further discouraged socializing with other tenants. They were, then, less likely to make efforts to find out about matters that were not satisfactorily explained by Jerry. In short, the tenants were poorly equipped to break down the pattern of isolation which appeared to largely define their social situation in the project.

The isolation of the tenants not only provided Jerry with an opportunity to manipulate them without fear of being discovered; it also made the tenants prey to those who showed promise of alleviating their problems or diminishing their loneliness. George remarked that he purposely spoke to female tenants at the door rather than entering their apartments in order to avoid embarrassing situations. He believed that the circumstances of their lives made them "man hungry." For some women, then, the friendly overtures or sexual favors of a man could be traded off for their willingness to remain on strike.

So far, we have seen how three factors fostered a pattern that socially and politically excluded the strikers from the rent strike: the way in which NAC organized its resources, the character of tenant relationships, and the characteristics of the tenants themselves. We have learned how this permitted and encouraged NAC not to inform or to misinform tenants on matters concerning the strike. These same factors, moreover, structured an approach toward tenants based upon relating largely to their fears, loneliness, and antagonism toward each other.

Tenants naturally feared eviction. NAC might have attempted to overcome these anxieties by bringing the strikers together and keeping them informed. The organizers might also have been able to reduce the alienation of these tenants by providing them with opportunities to act concertedly. But instead they exacerbated their isolation, which in turn increased their fears and left untouched the fragmented character of their social relationships. The tenants had no way of accurately learning how many other tenants were in "the same boat." Except for their contact with Jerry, there was no regular vehicle to reassure them that they would be protected against evictions. When Jerry confronted tenants, he necessarily had to relate to the enormous fears they expressed about the dangers of being on strike. In short, while the isolation of the tenants provided him with considerable latitude, it also favored the employment of certain strategies rather than others.

Jerry had a theory on how to organize, which he expressed on several occasions. In his own words, "anything goes" and "you gotta bullshit." But although he appeared willing to bend his strategy in any way necessary to maintain the strike, the kind of "bullshit" he employed was structured along the lines already indicated. That is, when making the rounds with Jerry to see the tenants, it became clear that considerable effort was focused on coping with their fears.

In attempting to reduce fears of eviction, Jerry grossly exaggerated the number of tenants on strike. He generally insisted, "over 300 tenants like you are on strike, and you know, more are joining every day." He would occasionally vary his estimates of the number of strikers, which suggested a greater concern with spicing up his line than with worrying that his inconsistencies would be discovered. He assumed, quite correctly, that the tenants would not be in contact with each other. He also insisted that NAC would never permit evictions to occur. They would demonstrate, sit in, and do whatever else was necessary to block the Housing Authority. He continually reminded tenants of how he and others had formerly stopped an eviction in Rogers Point: when the sheriff arrived with the moving van, he, along with others, successfully contacted more than 100 tenants to sit in.

But the political situation was very different now. The Housing Authority would not attempt an eviction unless they planned to carry it through. They had learned their lesson. Later on, during the strike, when there were indications that the Housing Authority was setting eviction procedures in motion, NAC became quite concerned. None of the organizers really felt the sense of certainty about halting an eviction that Jerry expressed to the tenants. Of course, there was no question that he would sincerely try to avert an attempted eviction. But Jerry also realized that he was overstating his case. Even though he admitted privately that he was worried, it was an important aspect of his organizing strategy never to show doubt about such matters before the tenants.

But while Jerry could successfully reduce some tenant fears about the strike, he would also exacerbate them for the purpose of preventing defections from the strike. It seemed to him that the most effective way to deal with someone's fears was to stir up or create other fears that were even greater. When reminding tenants of the deficiencies within their premises, he would tend to select items that were especially hazardous to their safety or that of their children. The following instance illustrates how he employed this device with an obviously fearful tenant who wanted to quit the strike.

> Mrs. F: But I got no complaints, Jerry. They come when I call.
>
> Jerry: What do y'mean, no complaints. Look at this. You wanna be robbed?
> (He then proceeded to borrow a hanger, leave the house, and lock the door. Through the mail slot at the bottom of the door, he artfully passed a bent hanger up to the door knob, and was thus able to open the door from the outside.)
>
> Jerry: If you don't want any stranger in your house in the middle of the night you better stay on strike. 'Cause we're gonna take care of that.

Jerry was attempting to counterbalance the tenant's fear of eviction with the presumably greater dangers facing her if drastic changes were not brought about. In another apartment, he stressed the hazards created by a tenant's tilted stove; children could be scalded by a pot of boiling water sliding off. Another emotionally laden issue that Jerry successfully exploited was fear of rats; he warned tenants of the danger that their children could suffer a fatal rat bite. To cite one more example, tenants very much wanted fresh paint jobs in their homes; they wanted attractive and clean-looking apartments. But when speaking to the tenants, Jerry stressed not the esthetic issues, but emphasized instead the danger of fungus growth resulting from the Housing

Authority's failure to paint frequently enough. When confronting their enormous resistance to remaining on strike, he thought his appeals to them had to be highly dramatic.

Jerry was so concerned about effect that he often included charges against the Housing Authority that were not accurate or even relevant to the demands that NAC was making. A stranger might be able to gain entrance to some apartments by using a hanger, but NAC never indicated this in its demands to the Housing Authority. As for the danger of rats, the current extermination program was among the very few policies of the Housing Authority approved by NAC. Yet when speaking to the tenants, Jerry referred to the Housing Authority's extermination program as just "propaganda."

One strategy that Jerry spoke proudly about was playing one tenant off against another. Its effective use depended upon an intimate familiarity with the community, which included knowing which tenants in particular disliked each other. He would stress to wavering tenants that people they detested were opposed to the strike. Jerry described this technique as follows:

Jerry: I would tell her (Mrs. X), "You know, Mrs. Y. said this strike is the stupidest thing she ever heard of, and she wouldn't join if this is the last thing she ever did." That would get her steaming mad, and keep her going on the strike for a while.

Myself: Did Mrs. Y. actually have any criticism of the strike?

Jerry: That's me talking, not her. The next day I went to see Mrs. Y. and told her Mrs. X was saying nasty things about the strike. She was thinking of joining, but that signed her up on the spot.

There were certainly other considerations that accounted for these tenants joining the strike, but it is indicative of its character that two tenants could be involved partly because each believed that the other was hostile to it. Since they did not talk to each other, presumably had no mutual friends, and there were no NAC meetings for them to attend, Jerry chanced that they would not discover each other's participation in the rent strike.

As the above discussion suggests, these were lonely people, and Jerry was able to capitalize upon this as well. Certainly, for many of these tenants, he offered the only regular contact they had with anyone. Being isolated and lonely, Jerry's friendship and interest in their welfare was most welcome. For some tenants, his regular calls must have provided sufficient incentive to remain on strike. To defect from the rent strike might mean that Jerry would not be knocking at their doors anymore.

With several striking tenants, his encounters were intimate. Throughout the strike, Jerry was engaging in a number of sexual affairs. Though these relationships were not intended as organizing strategies, such entanglements had consequences for the character of the strike. Jerry had regular and frequent contact with these strikers, who were often without boy friends of their own. Being mothers with considerable time and energy invested in their children, scouting for male companionship was difficult. Also, the physical isolation of Rogers Point from any kind of social facilities further inhibited their opportunities for meeting men.

Resisting affairs under circumstances that posed these temptations would require an unusual degree of self-restraint from almost any man. This is one important reason that George stood at the doorways and preferred not to have any close contact with women in the projects. Living in the Rogers Point project with a wife and ten children, he felt that extramarital affairs would destroy his leadership position in the community as well as adversely affect his personal life. George clearly understood the temptations that daily encounters with welfare mothers involved. Jerry did not reside in Rogers Point, and he was separated from his family. Also, he did not occupy the "higher" leadership position that George did. So, there was considerably less pull for him to resist temptations to conduct affairs with tenants.

But the demands and needs of these women conflicted with those of Jerry, and this tended to inject a high degree of instability and tension into these relationships. While their needs generally were considerably more than sexual, the sexual aspects of these affairs, with a minimum of other ties, was Jerry's primary interest. So even if he did not "naturally" tend to flit from one woman to another, the explosive character of these makeshift relationships would favor short-term encounters and numerous affairs. Since these women were not brought together in a common meeting place, Jerry was not restrained by the difficulties such a confrontation would have caused.

On the other hand, simply moving from one affair to another could have created cracks in the strike. There was the danger that a woman angry with Jerry might withdraw from participation. Since Jerry was committed to the strike, and in fact successfully prevented defections, it is likely that these sexual affairs were partly structured around the needs of the strike. Though I have no evidence to support this contention, I suspect that the pressures of his organizing role forced Jerry to flit not from one striker to another, but rather to shuttle back and forth. It seems that he had to maintain these relationships, even if only intermittently rather than regularly, in order for NAC to retain the loyalty of the strikers.

Though I never inquired how extensive these affairs were, three of them were known to me. One striker franti-

cally came to NAC's office looking for Jerry, who had not
been "home" the night before. On another occasion, I was
introduced to the children of his newly acquired girl friend,
who was also on strike. Still a third time, when asking my
assistance in clearing his police record, he provided me in
confidence, in case I had to reach him quickly, with the address and phone number of another striker with whom he
was temporarily living. These entanglements would have
made quitting the strike very difficult and extremely awkward for the tenants.

With at least some of the women, then, Jerry's relationship was much more extensive than implied in his role as
organizer. There were occasions when he would even bor-
row money from them to meet alimony payments and other
expenses. However, his leverage with the strikers rested in
part upon his economic independence from them. He was
not just an unemployed boyfriend or "moocher," but
earned his own living. For these women, participation in
the rent strike was a small price to pay for obtaining a boyfriend.

So Jerry manipulated them in the service of his own
needs as well as those of the rent strike. The result was to
further commit Jerry and NAC to assuring that the tenants
remain isolated from each other. Conducting meetings with
tenants would involve grave risks, as Jerry clearly understood:

> Me: Jerry, wouldn't it be a good idea to meet with the
> tenants?
>
> Jerry: We have meetings all the time. I meet with them
> every day, in their homes.
>
> Me: But what about bringing them together at the office?
>
> Jerry: Do you think I'm crazy! They'd be after my scalp.

Concerted hostility of the strikers toward Jerry, which might have resulted from bringing these mothers into contact with each other, could also have been converted into antagonism toward the strike itself. The isolation of the tenants from each other, which initially reflected the orientation and character of NAC, became a necessary expedient.

Not only were meetings avoided, but the strikers were not invited to picket with NAC or to join delegations sent to the Housing Authority. It is not that the exclusion of tenants from these public gatherings always reflected deliberate efforts to avoid embarrassment and complications. For Jerry, the avoidance of such collective encounters was quite deliberate. But for NAC as a whole, the conception of the tenants' role as limited to the withholding of rent rendered them irrelevant for any other purpose.

III

The organizers frequently stressed the importance of involving the poor in the battle against poverty, and they often justified a plan of action on the basis that it expressed the desires of the tenants. Moreover, they said a great deal about the importance of respecting black women, whom they claimed had been taken advantage of for too long. Yet clearly, they did not involve tenants even on the most elementary level of providing them with accurate information. As other observers became aware of the disparity between what they said and how they behaved, the organizers were often called hypocrites who were cynically exploiting the tenants for their own interests.

But in truth, they were genuinely devoted to the cause of the strike, which was to improve living conditions for the tenants. None of them believed that their participation in the strike represented a form of self-aggrandizement. On the contrary, they believed themselves to be self-sacrificing.

So the view of some that they were "hypocrites" understandably did not describe how they viewed themselves. They would become profoundly insulted at any insinuations that they were insincere. They saw themselves as behaving democratically and respectfully toward the tenants.

The organizers were able to maintain this image of their conduct largely because they did not draw sharp lines between their behavior and their ideological claims. There was evidence to show that for them the word was often equivalent to the deed. To sound militant was to be militant. To proclaim democratic sentiments was to be democratic. When Curtis Jones, for example, would address himself to such crucial issues as "militancy" or "democratic participation" in the strike, his facial muscles would tighten and his eyes would assume an unusual intensity. His demeanor would suggest considerable pride and sense of self-importance. Unless he was engaged in battle or otherwise engrossed, he generally seemed depressed and somewhat lost. His eyes would not appear fixed upon any point in his setting, whether a person or object, but, instead, seemed turned inward. On these occasions, however, they became focused. So the transformation that took place during intense discussions about his beliefs became strikingly visible. In short, he seemed to come alive.

This apparent resurrection from depression to "liveness" must have corresponded to a leap from the experiencing of emptiness to the world of relatedness. In other words, the symbolic impact of these rhetorical flights released and stirred a flood of images that were experienced as extremely gratifying. Curtis felt alive and real, which in turn gave liveness and reality to his images. Under these circumstances, it is understandable that the "word" becomes the "deed," and accordingly that to proclaim commitment to democratic norms was subjectively experienced as actual commitment to them.

A gap between how individuals actually behave politically and their political self-image is not uncommon. In these organizers the gap was conspicuous and great. It appears that they shaped their self-images not primarily on the basis of their responses to current social situations, but rather through the interlacing of fantasies about themselves, which were then socially projected. So the arena in which they operated provided primarily the stage from which to project their idealized images rather than being mainly a source for shaping and reshaping internal experience.

In short, they were not behaving "hypocritically," as many claimed. They were not attempting to "put over" anything on the tenants; from their viewpoint, they really wanted to improve housing conditions. What is more, they tended to regard their involvement in tenant affairs as a self-sacrifice. What Curtis and the others believed really did exist for them and became defined as real. So when discussing their political philosophy, they had reason to maintain considerable pride and confidence in their own integrity.

CHAPTER FOUR

NAC AND THE ESTABLISHMENT

THE NEIGHBORHOOD Action Committee's relationship to the Housing Authority and other establishment contacts contained striking parallels to Jerry Cook's relationship to the tenants. Just as putting on the tenants was the main vehicle for retaining their allegiance, NAC attempted to win the strike primarily by putting on the establishment. Specifically, they were convinced that by creating an illusion of their power, the Housing Authority could eventually be intimidated into making major concessions. Let us see why the organizers adopted this strategy, how they proceeded to implement it, and what consequences followed.

The black nationalist political philosophy of NAC tended to isolate the organization from potential and actual sources of support. Unlike the leadership of the South Peak Tenants Union, which was also conducting a rent strike, the organizers at Rogers Point did not believe that major concessions could be obtained from the establishment by making alliances with white middle-class citizens. Curtis Jones, whose politics dominated NAC, considered himself a staunch black power advocate. By black power, he meant essentially the use of direct action strategies exclusively by black people for their own benefit. He believed that only through the flexing of black political muscle could white-controlled institutions be compelled to adopt programs favorable to blacks.

Curtis adamantly opposed forming alliances with whites. First, he believed that any gains made by such coalitions were bound to be offset by compromises injurious to black people. Second, he thought these coalitions would invariably lead to white domination of black politics, whereas he believed that black people must develop political experience and confidence, which would be considerably inhibited, if not nullified, by cooperating with white citizens.

Curtis therefore believed that alliances with whites could only result in the undermining of the goals and strategies of blacks. For this reason, he did not generally draw any distinctions between various whites representing different political positions and groups. For example, he believed that the Housing Authority or white establishment was guilty of maintaining slum conditions. Those whites seemingly opposed to these practices were thought to be attempting "to cool off" black people or operating with other questionable motives in mind. One white differed from another only in terms of how he implemented racist practices. All whites were accordingly defined as opponents, and alliances against the power structure were restricted essentially to other blacks.

According to Curtis Jones' strategy for battling the establishment, organizing a massive rent strike and engaging in militant activities would be sufficient to force the Housing Authority to drastically improve conditions. Curtis had hoped that the city-wide Presentation City Tenant Council would serve as a vehicle for coordinating such activities throughout the City. But, as we have noted, it was essentially a paper organization. Its new president, Roy Smith, was leading a rent strike in a public housing project, but there were only six participants and even so he had no interest in enlarging the strike. Roy was no militant, which made any meaningful cooperation with him extremely difficult for Curtis.

The only other viable tenants organization was the South Peak Tenants Union. But it was opposed to allying with either the city-wide tenant organization or the Rogers Point organizers, whom it considered "too far out in left field." In any case, NAC decried their moderate approach as well. The organizers strongly opposed cooperating with other blacks at the expense of tempering their radicalism or diluting NAC's militant style. In general, what many other black leaders would have considered realistic compromises, they defined as "selling out." These various factors, then, including the weakness of tenant organizations in Presentation City and NAC's ideology, tended to politically isolate NAC from the rest of the Presentation City community.

An alternative available to NAC was to develop substantial tenant participation within their own project. They were convinced that a massive rent strike in Rogers Point would be an effective strategy, and such a direct action campaign would certainly have been in accord with their political philosophy. However, for reasons already stated, most particularly the way in which NAC deployed its resources, they were most unlikely to substantially increase the number of tenants on strike.

So the organizers were trapped in a dilemma that they both inherited and created. Social conditions, their radical, militant, nationalist ideology, and the organizers' own style of operation frustrated their bid for influence and power. The organizers responded in terms of the only option that seemed available to them: if they lacked power, they would create an illusion of power. They assumed that if the Housing Authority could be convinced that NAC possessed considerable power, this would be tantamount to actually wielding power and the Housing Authority would ultimately be forced to capitulate. NAC's attempt to create an illusion of power consisted of three basic strategies: exag-

gerating the number of strikers; implying widespread con-
nections with other black militant organizations; and,
issuing threats against the Housing Authority and its allies.
One or more of these strategies were employed during each
of four successive stages of the strike.

During the initial stage, or the first several months of
the rent strike, NAC had no contact with the Housing
Authority or any other public official or agency. The organizers deliberately avoided any encounters because they
were convinced that nothing would be gained until the
Housing Authority "realized" that it was dealing with a
formidable organization. Since they had no contact with
the Housing Authority, they necessarily relied on indirect
means of communications to convey "the message." They
issued press releases and spoke frequently about their activities to others, trusting that the Housing Authority would
learn about them sooner or later.

They also held informational picket lines in front of
City Hall, and spoke with numerous other citizens whom
they believed had a grapevine to the agency. Their lack of
direct contact with the Housing Authority probably minimized any reluctance they might have had about exaggerating their strength. The indirect line of communication
made their boasts unofficial, and also made them less prone
to speculate about the possible adverse consequences of this
strategy. They did not consider, for example, that discovery
of their ruse might cause others not to take them seriously in
the future.

Unlike the relatively precise estimate given to the
tenants of the number of rent strikers, as 300 or 350, NAC's
public exaggeration tended to be vague and qualitative. Ex-
amples of their boasts included "It's spreading like wild
fire," "It's tripled in the last few weeks," "Most of them will
be joined up soon," "It looks like the other projects are com-

ing in fast," "It's gotten so tenants are feeling queer paying their rents." NAC occasionally claimed at this early stage of the strike that "hundreds are striking," but without indicating precisely how many hundreds.

There was one notable exception to their vague and general overstatements. Various persons who were considered by the organizers as allies were offered, like project tenants, relatively precise rather than vague estimates. But these too were always exaggerated. For example, NAC told one of its lawyers and me that the strike had grown to include 150 tenants. Since we were assisting them, they responded to "our right to know." NAC interpreted this to mean that they were obligated to offer us a specific number, but not necessarily an accurate one. But, on the whole, their exaggerations tended to be qualitative. Other individuals were flatly refused more precise information on the basis that they were outsiders, and therefore could not be "let in" on organizational secrets. In any case, NAC believed it was accomplishing its task of getting the Housing Authority to learn of its presumed strength.

The organizers did have a basis for believing that the actual number of strikers could not be readily discovered by the Housing Authority. First, they did not reveal the actual number of tenants whom they recruited to strike. Striking tenants had been instructed to obtain money orders made out to the Housing Authority. But unlike the South Peak Tenants Union, which was also on strike, they opened no bank account to show the Housing Authority. Instead, NAC placed these checks in a bank vault whose location was known only to themselves. Second, whether or not tenants were striking, each month a considerable number of them did not pay their rent. About two weeks later, the assistant manager of each housing project would personally deliver to each of these tenants a "three-day notice," a legal warning to pay rent immediately or become subject to eviction proceedings. The Housing Authority was delivering on the average of 250 three-day notices each month in Rogers Point. When the strike first began, there was no way of determining from the statistics of rent delinquency how many of them were actually participating.

The rent strike leaders assumed that this massive tardiness would obscure the actual number of strike participants from the Housing Authority. However, they did not consider that the overwhelming majority of delinquent tenants did pay their rent almost immediately after receiving their three-day notice. A large rent strike would be reflected in a greater number of tenants withholding their rents regularly; in other words, the same 250 tenants would not be withholding their rents each month unless they were on strike or were otherwise chronic delinquents. But those who failed to pay their rents over a long period of time constituted a very small percentage of tenants, which the carefully kept records of the Housing Authority clearly showed.

Furthermore, the Housing Authority staff located at Rogers Point routinely investigated rent delinquency in the project, and provided the main office with data on why tenants persistently deliquent were tardy in their rent payments. Even if the Housing Authority's records were not entirely accurate, their margin of error was bound to be too small to make credible the inflated claims of NAC. When these observations were mentioned to George Franklyn, he responded with considerable surprise. The organizers had not considered the risks of being discovered.

In addition to exaggerating their strength, they frequently threatened massive action such as demonstrations and sit-ins. They also repeatedly warned of possible riots. George was fond of saying, "There's been no riot in Rogers Point, but you know, there's always a first time." The organizers often mentioned they had once averted a riot in their community but were not sure they would do so again. The implications of these remarks were clear. The organizers did not suggest that they would directly touch off a disturbance, but instead implied that they were in an excellent position to stop one. They were claiming, in fact, that their wide-spread contact with discontented residents in the community was keeping the lid on riots and the crime rate in general.

The organizers assumed that these various forebodings would reach the Housing Authority and the mayor's office. They were claiming not only a substantial and increasing number of tenants were striking, but also that they were in a position to engage in massive direct action campaigns. They had hoped that the Housing Authority would be impressed with their allegedly large following and the potential manpower that they could draw upon, which was implied in their many sweeping assertions. In actuality, their strike was small and the organizers were in no position to rally widespread support. But somehow they still expected that their militant threats would force the establishment to initiate contacts with them and negotiate their grievances. They were soon to establish contact with the Housing Authority, though on terms that were both surprising and unfavorable to them.

During the next stage of the strike, the scene of battle shifted to the courtroom. Tenants who did not acknowledge the three-day notices were served with summonses to appear in court. The Housing Authority was legally required to obtain a court order before evicting anyone. The tenants panicked. Most of them demanded that NAC return their rent money so that they could withdraw from the strike. The pressure was not applied only on Jerry; many tenants also contacted the NAC office to speak to the other organizers, particularly Curtis Jones.

The organizers promised them that they would not tolerate evictions. But the tenants did not feel reassured and neither, really, did the organizers, who also panicked. To prevent the rent strike from falling apart, they contacted the City's OEO legal service program to procure free legal defense for the tenants. Jerry brought one of the lawyers to meet briefly with the tenants to assure them that they would be legally protected. In this way, NAC successfully averted wholesale defection from the rent strike.

But in meeting the Housing Authority's challenge, they committed themselves to waging a defensive court battle, which was to consume much of their time and energy for several months. NAC could have obtained a mass trial for their tenants, as the South Peak Tenants Union had requested for publicity purposes. But the organizers saw a grave risk in this, because losing a single trial could have subjected all the striking tenants to almost immediate eviction. Instead, they preferred to stretch the legal battle over an extended period of time in order to prolong the strike and deter evictions. The counsel for the Housing Authority was agreeable to their request that "everybody deserves his day in court." The Housing Authority also preferred to avoid the adverse publicity that a mass trial might have received.

Although there were organizing advantages to prolonging the legal battle with the Housing Authority, there was also a serious danger in it. Still not appreciating that the Housing Authority kept fairly accurate records, the organizers continued to believe that only they themselves were aware of the actual number of strikers. Accordingly, they feared that the court proceedings would provide an opportunity for the Housing Authority to learn what, in fact, they already knew—their actual strength. By simply counting the number of tenants NAC brought to court for trial, the Housing Authority could assume, unless other considerations were called to their attention, that these individuals constituted virtually the entire number of strikers. From NAC's point of view, they could avoid this risk by simply deciding that the tenants should not appear. On the whole, tenants rarely answered summonses. But as the organizers realized, not appearing for trial could have hastened eviction proceedings. So NAC took what it considered the chance of being discovered, and brought virtually all the strikers to court. The strikers were regularly accompanied to court by all four organizers. Jerry Cook normally did not join the others outside the community, but since he was in charge of the tenants, the responsibility of assuring that they appeared rested primarily on his shoulders.

The organizers employed two strategies at this stage to impress the Housing Authority that it was dealing with a formidable group. First, they repeatedly claimed that only a few of the striking tenants who were receiving summonses had decided to appear in court. Of course, those tenants who came to court could conceivably have constituted a small percentage of those on strike. But the organizers were mistakenly assuming that the Housing Authority could determine the number of strikers only by literally seeing them. At these court hearings, three officers of the agency appeared: the assistant manager of Rogers Point, the assistant manager of rent collections, and the Housing Authority's attorney. All three of these officials were well informed. They knew the organizers were bluffing and made various remarks to indicate that they were not being deceived. As the trials proceeded from one week to another, the organizers became at least dimly aware that their ruse was unsuccessful.

The second major strategy to intimidate opponents was to imply through dress and demeanor that the organizers were linked to a large and militant black nationalist movement. To understand the character of this strategy requires some background discussion, for it was not initially intended as a means to alarm the establishment. Under the leadership of Curtis Jones, the prevailing mood of black unity and opposition to the white community crystallized into a black nationalist cult. Together, the organizers studied African history, asserted an African heritage by attempting to learn Swahili, adopted African names, which they prominently displayed on signs in the local office, and traced their ancestry to African tribes. Most conspicuous to others, they often wore African clothing. These included hats (tarboosh), decorated shirts, sandals, and necklaces holding a carved Negroid face, which they claimed represented the first man. Curtis' garments were even more elaborate, and occasionally included a full-length shawl (caftah). This appeared to symbolically represent his leadership over the other organizers.

The changing meaning of these symbols over a period of time indicated the enormous influence of Curtis Jones. For example, the organizers claimed that the hat was a symbol of authority and should be worn whenever they were asserting themselves and making decisions. For this reason, they at first wore the hats during working hours. Later, they were no longer used regularly. There was one important exception, however: the organizers always wore them when engaging in political battles with non-blacks. In this regard, they were following Curtis, for it was this aspect of authority, the confronting of white opposition, which was most compelling to him and therefore to the other organizers. So this symbol of male authority, which at first reflected a generalized role, became essentially a symbol of opposition to other racial groups, particularly members of the white establishment.

With the considerable attention given by the media and the public to the presumably dangerous character of black nationalist groups, the organizers concluded that African clothing, appropriately used, could have a political function. It could convey to their opponents the impression that they were members of an awesome organization of black nationalists. They believed that their non-black enemies could be frightened by the thought of "hordes of blacks" organized for concerted action against them. In their battles with the Mexican leaders of the Granada poverty program, they thought that attending meetings fully dressed in African garb and engaging in such practices as calling each other by their African names successfully intimidated the Mexicans. They also believed that this would be an effective strategy against the white establishment.

They did not behave as convincingly as they believed, and this strategy backfired. With the exception of Curtis, who carried himself with considerable dignity, the behavior of the organizers was often transparent. For example, with a very conspicuous deadpan pose, they would loudly call each other by their African names. Or they would deliberately stare simultaneously at one official for the purpose of frightening him. The response of the Housing Authority officials to such behavior was to consider the organizers "nice but silly kids," though they regarded Curtis as mainly responsible for "misleading" the others. Interestingly enough, two of these "nice kids," George and Jerry, were ages thirty-four and thirty-seven years old, respectively.

NAC never clarified for the establishment what actual dangers they should fear from the presumed alliance with other militant blacks. Actually, some of the organizers maintained informal contact with members of the Black Panther Party, but these contacts were highly secretive, and to my knowledge the organizers never had any intention of involving members of the Panthers in their battle against the Housing Authority. Rather, they somehow believed that their demeanor would be sufficient to convince the establisehment of their powers and to ultimately intimidate them into making concessions.

The third stage of the strike consisted of public confrontations with the establishment, which in contrast to the courtroom scenes, the organizers themselves initiated and aggressively pursued. Through its contact with the citywide Presentation City Tenant Council, NAC put together a delegation of fifteen persons to demand a meeting with the mayor. They had lost their court cases, which gave the Housing Authority legal license to evict the striking tenants. NAC understood that the evictions would be postponed until after the mayoralty elections, but these were only a few months away. The organizers believed that it was important for NAC to move as swiftly as possible to achieve its aims. Their plan of action was to present and discuss with the mayor a detailed list of their grievances against the Housing Authority. With the election approaching, they thought that the potential threat of militant activities if their grievances were not met would make the mayor more sensitive to their demands.

The fifteen delegates met together in the lobby of City Hall about a half-hour before entering the mayor's office. None of them represented formidable organizations, but several claimed they did when questioned by reporters who were present. Some said they represented other public housing tenant organizations which were also prepared to act strongly against the Housing Authority. A few delegates were members of organizations but had no authorization to represent them; they spoke as authorized representatives anyway. Two others actually invented names of organizations which they presumably represented. This ruse was thought up a few minutes before they talked with reporters.

The delegation entered the lobby of the mayor's office

and was greeted by Paul Brooks, his Housing Coordinator. Curtis at once demanded a meeting with the mayor to discuss tenant problems in public housing. Brooks told them that he was officially representing the mayor and would be happy to discuss their problems. (He was thought to be the mayor's right-hand man, but the extent of his actual influence over him was not altogether clear.) Though Brooks was known to Curtis, he was understandably uncertain of how Brooks could possibly assist the strikers. At the moment, Curtis interpreted his intervention as simply a dodge on the part of the mayor. He politely thanked him for his interest, but indicated that the delegation was there to see only the mayor. He said that the urgent concerns of the delegation required that they meet with the chief executive of the City now, and that they had no intention of leaving the office until they had done so. Brooks insisted that the mayor's schedule was extremely busy that day, for he had just returned from the airport where he had greeted the Imperial family of Japan and now there were other individuals and delegations waiting to see him. Curtis responded, "It's about time he meets the imperial people of Presentation City." The other members of the delegation were obviously pleased with this retort.

A thick circle of people crowded around Curtis and Brooks. The inner circle included the delegation and a representative from the Housing Authority who was informally present. Other onlookers in the lobby of the mayor's office crowded also around. Curtis finally convinced Brooks that he was serious and would not leave until some concession had been made. Brooks then left for a couple of minutes to see the mayor, and during this interim Curtis was flooded with compliments by members of the delegation for displaying political astuteness and "standing up" to Brooks. Brooks returned with an appointment set for the following week.

The delegation appeared satisfied, and it seemed that Curtis had won a victory.

But Curtis was not placated. He had committed himself to obtaining an immediate session with the mayor, and he thought acceptance of Brooks' compromise would be a complete submission to the mayor's terms, both in a personal and a political sense. He told Brooks that this arrangement was still unacceptable, and then repeated the threat that the delegation would not leave until the mayor met with them. The following exchange ensued between Brooks and Curtis:

> Brooks: The mayor is really busy, but will be happy to speak with your delegation next week.

> Curtis: But all we really want is a few minutes now. The mayor can certainly spare two minutes.

Curtis was engaged in a tug of war with Brooks. Right after this exchange, another member of the delegation, with the obvious approval of the others, intruded for the first time. Taking Curtis aside, he told him that the arrangement was really quite satisfactory and that a full hour later would be much better than only a few minutes now. Curtis then complied, saying that he would accede to the consensus of the group. He might have thought the delegation could extend two minutes into an hour or more, but he certainly gave no such indications to the others. Rather, in a rare display of modesty, he apologized to the others on the way out for behaving unwisely, but added that he didn't like those "punks" to get away with things. He apparently realized that he had trapped himself into ignoring the main purpose of arranging a meeting with the mayor, and that staging a sit-in then would have been politically premature and inappropriate.

Certainly, a major explanation for his behavior was fear

of losing face. Though aware that a strategic retreat was the most politically advisable move, it did not serve his self-interest in the psychological sense. Not having obtained all his demands seemed tantamount to surrender, which suggested to him cowardice. This particular political situation played into these feelings. The political experience of black people has taught many of them that delays by the establishment often mean doing nothing about alleviating social and economic problems. For a black leader such as Curtis, then, to "give in" may seem like "giving up." Whatever justification there may be for such a historical interpretation of black-white relations, there is a tendency among many blacks to apply this historically induced response inappropriately. That seems to have been the case in this instance, for had Curtis followed his instincts it might have produced a political calamity.

During the meeting with the mayor the following week, top-ranking members of the Housing Authority also appeared. The organizers had been informed that agency representatives were being invited and they made no objections. When the meeting began, Curtis attempted to "expose" the evils of the Housing Authority by making accusations and questioning the motives of the Housing Authority administrators. The agency representatives at first sat quietly as Curtis, in effect, presented NAC's demands to the mayor. The mayor urged NAC to meet with agency officials to discuss their complaints. He granted that they had legitimate concerns, but he claimed that their problems could not be resolved by bypassing the Housing Authority. Curtis and the other organizers who joined in continued to attack the agency, claiming that it refused to cooperate in dealing with NAC. The mayor then told O'Rourke that he should make a serious attempt to discuss NAC's grievances with them. By this time, the Housing Authority administrators were responding defensively and soon almost everyone was shouting at each other. The meeting was falling apart.

Finally, a black OEO legal services attorney, invited by the organizers to join them, suggested that the present atmosphere offered no opportunity for reconciling differences. Instead, he urged the Housing Authority officials to meet in Rogers Point, where the tenants themselves would be able to attend, to consider the various grievances. O'Rourke, the executive director of the Housing Authority, indicated that his agency had always been willing to talk with any tenant group and would certainly be willing to meet with NAC at the project. A meeting in Rogers Point was set up for two weeks later.

Before meeting with the Housing Authority, NAC and several members of the city-wide Presentation City Tenant Council met to draw up demands. They agreed that their first demand should be a continued moratorium on evictions while negotiations were being conducted. Curtis insisted upon making this demand an ultimatum, with the meeting to be called off unless it was accepted. One member from the city-wide tenant group argued that even if the Housing Authority should reject this demand, the remainder of their grievances should be presented to determine the extent to which it appeared willing to make concessions; then the tenant leaders could decide whether further negotiations were warranted. But this proposal, which Curtis vehemently opposed as "selling out the tenants," was voted down.

The public meeting with the Housing Authority at Rogers Point was attended by newspaper reporters, news representatives from the major television channels, and a few tenants. Lawyers from the City's OEO legal service program attended, but only as onlookers; NAC would not permit them to participate in the negotiations. At the negotiation table sat the NAC organizers and one Tenant Council delegate from another project. The Housing Authority was represented by its top administrators. O'Rourke acted as the chief spokesman during what turned out to be a very brief meeting.

The first demand, for a longer moratorium on evictions, was offered by the same member who had opposed it. As he had said earlier to the others, he believed that a display of unity among rent strike leaders deserved precedence over all other considerations; nor did he want to be labelled an "Uncle Tom." O'Rourke countered with two different responses. First, he reacted to the implication, which he correctly read into the remarks, that the Tenant Council or NAC represented and could speak for all the tenants. Though he indicated his willingness to talk with them about tenant grievances, he refused to acknowledge them as an official bargaining agent. He said that the organizers had offered no evidence to convince the Housing Authority that they actually did represent a large proportion of the tenants, and that in any case it was not considered expedient by the Housing Authority to designate any single group as an exclusive bargaining agent.

Second, and most important, he clearly implied that there were no plans in the immediate future to evict tenants. O'Rourke stopped short of explicitly confirming the Housing Authority's current non-eviction policy because he feared that many tenants would interpret this as a license to stop paying rent. Without an explicit guarantee, Curtis and the other organizers could not be appeased. The following exchange occurred:

> O'Rourke: I repeat, the facts speak for themselves. We have not been attempting any evictions.
>
> Curtis: You must certainly understand our position. We cannot proceed with negotiations without assurances that no tenants will be evicted.

O'Rourke: I cannot give any guarantees. But again I repeat.
The facts speak for themselves. We have not been
evicting anybody. Let's continue with the meeting.

George then interjected:

George: Negotiations wouldn't take more than a month.
I don't understand your attitude, O'Rourke.
We're making a reasonable request. . . .

Both the tone and content of O'Rourke's remarks suggested to members of the audience, including the legal staff
and reporters, that no evictions would occur. Even aside
from his reassuring comments, virtually no one familiar with
this issue believed that the Housing Authority would proceed soon with evictions. It was already the month of May,
and officials of the Housing Authority realized that tensions
in the ghetto communities would probably be increasing
through the summer months. An eviction around this time
would be most unwise. Also, only a few months were left before the mayoralty elections, and it was generally believed
that no matter what machinery the Housing Authority set in
motion, no evictions would be attempted until after then.

But the organizers would accept nothing less than an
explicit promise from O'Rourke that he would continue the
moratorium on evictions. They abruptly brought the meeting to an end, only about ten minutes after it began. Immediately afterwards, the organizers returned to their office.
Curtis was proud that they had stood up to the Housing
Authority, noting that NAC had set its own terms for negotiations and had brought the meeting to an end when the
Housing Authority would not accede. All the NAC organizers appeared to be in good spirits, enjoying what seemed
to them a victory.

I asked Curtis then whether he would consider it worthwhile to demonstrate to the Housing Authority that they represented most of the tenants in Rogers Point by obtaining their signatures on a petition. I argued that such a strategy would, at the least, bring NAC considerable publicity and provide political advantages for it in dealings with the Housing Authority. It would also provide the agency with some concrete evidence that NAC was not acting on behalf of only a small group. Though most tenants would not actually strike, convincing them to sign a petition endorsing NAC as their bargaining agent would have been a relatively easy task. Curtis categorically rejected this strategy on the grounds that it would be tantamount to conducting the strike on the establishment's terms. It was not their task to demonstrate the legitimacy of their organization to the Housing Authority, he said; to do so would be an indication of weakness, and therefore tactically unwise.

For the organizers, and particularly Curtis, the distinction between "doing things our way or theirs" seemed crucial. Feelings of pride and independence, an unwillingness to be thought of as Uncle Toms, seemed to make them extremely sensitive to permitting the Caucasian establishment to define the rules of the game. Adopting any strategies that were sanctioned by the establishment tended to be regarded by them as an abdication of their principles. Though they usually claimed political expediency as their guiding principle, such non-political factors frequently outweighed practical considerations.

Following the meeting at Rogers Point, there was a lull for several months. The organizers did attend a couple of public meetings of the Housing Authority Commission, but these were uneventful. During the summer Jerry continued his efforts to keep the strike going, but there were no other strike-related activities. After the summer, primarily through the intervention of a black commissioner, NAC was brought together for private meetings with top administrators of the Housing Authority. So the fourth and final period of the strike began. All the organizers, except Jerry, attended these meetings.

Concurrently, the organizers and the Housing Authority were meeting on a different matter. George wanted to develop facilities for young people in Rogers Point and asked O'Rourke for the use of an empty building in the project. O'Rourke then requested a social worker on his staff to investigate and submit his own impressions. He returned from a visit to the organizers' office convinced that they were militant black nationalists. He noted their African names on the walls, and saw militant posters in the window. He also spoke with them, which of course confirmed his impressions. Believing that they would use the building to advance their political cause, the social worker recommended that they not be allowed to use it.

But O'Rourke was apparently not as fearful of their presumed militancy. He thought that it might be possible to use their desire to obtain these quarters for his own political advantage. At the private negotiation meetings, he indicated that the Housing Authority would permit them the use of their facility, but as evidence of good faith, he wanted them to cease their activities. Not surprisingly, they refused. The organizers claimed that only when the Housing Authority would agree to all their demands would they end the strike.

However, NAC was really in a poor position to negotiate. Within the last several months, about one-third of the striking tenants had defected and were no longer turning over their rent money; they were spending it, instead, on personal needs. Also, pressure from the tenants to withdraw from the strike was increasing. So far, Jerry had flatly refused to return their rent money to them. But their insistence increased. In short, the strike was beginning to fall apart.

Meanwhile, the Housing Authority was implementing a landscape program in Rogers Point, which was made possible through special federal funds. Further, tenant complaints were being handled more promptly and courteously. When taking office, O'Rourke had promised to improve maintenance and repair services by streamlining their operation, and he had publicly announced that the Housing Authority was making plans to landscape the Rogers Point area, as promised to the tenants by his predecessor.

Though these were commitments that O'Rourke had made before the strike, NAC attributed these plans solely to their own efforts. In fact, as soon as landscaping activities began, Jerry reminded striking tenants that this development was concrete evidence of the value of the strike. In fact, the organizers really did believe that the landscaping program reflected the effectiveness of their organization. I reminded them that the program, including the allocation of federal funds and the approximate date it would begin, had been announced before their strike. Curtis retorted that the Housing Authority would never have kept its promise without a rent strike in the project; the organizers could not imagine it making any improvements voluntarily.

In any case, an increasing number of tenants wanted their money returned. The demand for Jerry's companionship seemed to be diminishing, and distrust of the organizers increasing. Though this situation made NAC more vulnerable politically, Curtis still insisted on maintaining the strike until the Housing Authority capitulated. He still believed that NAC could successfully overstate the number of striking tenants, and convince the Authority that it faced a powerful opponent. Without paying careful attention to their earlier experience of making overstatements, they now believed that the growing debt provided them with a subterfuge which would prevent their real strength from being discovered, for it meant, in part, that more tenants were becoming delinquent in paying rent, and that NAC could therefore claim that many of them had joined the strike.

Further, they were convinced that their claim to a larger following than they really had was not too great a distortion of the facts. As a result of the Housing Authority's non-eviction policy, more tenants were becoming delinquent in rent payments and Housing Authority's deficit climbed. The difficult financial situation of the agency received widespread notice in the press. Actually, the Housing Authority deliberately issued press releases reporting their rapidly deteriorating financial condition in order to prepare the public for its plans to end the moratorium on eviction. When NAC learned about the Housing Authority's problems, they concluded that their rent strike, and the publicity given to it, primarily accounted for the Housing Authority's fiscal problems. Many tenants were being inspired, they believed, by their example. Their deliberate exaggeration of the number of strikers, then, seemed valid to them.

I found it surprising that until then it had not occurred to NAC members that their strike was having greater impact upon the Housing Authority. It would have been easy to assume that other tenants were following their example, but this possibility had not even been suggested before. They assumed that tenants related to each other, if at all, only antagonistically—an assumption that shaped their organizing strategy.

But since an increasing number of tenants were not paying rent, they believed that they could imply during negotiations with the Housing Authority that they retained in their possession much more rent money than they actually had. They were not troubled by the thought that their scheme might backfire, because the Housing Authority would presumably not discover how much money they possessed until after the housing conditions were improved; according to their plans, only then would NAC return the rent money to the agency. So, ironically, despite the vulnerable position created by growing tenant antagonism toward them, the NAC organizers entered these private negotiations feeling strong and confident.

Officials of the Housing Authority, on the other hand, were no more convinced now than before of NAC's influence and power. O'Rourke's administration did maintain a policy of meeting with all tenant groups, and they were anxious to meet with NAC to settle the strike. But the strike was not viewed as having any substantial impact upon the Housing Authority's increasing debt. As before, they knew how many tenants were actually participating in the strike.

During these private negotiations between NAC and the Housing Authority, O'Rourke offered to investigate tenant complaints to determine the feasibility of answering them with appropriate repairs. He asked NAC for a list of strikers, together with the complaints each of them had about conditions. NAC refused to do so during the first several meetings, for the organizers believed that this was a ruse to discover their real strength. O'Rourke insisted that without such a list, he was in no position to verify their charges and actually see to it that improvements were made. NAC finally submitted a list.

O'Rourke gave it to the assistant manager of Rogers Point with orders to investigate swiftly and submit a report of his findings. NAC had kept a file of tenant grievances in its office, and it was from these files that the list of tenant complaints was drawn up. Unfortunately, the list had not been brought up to date. Perhaps the organizers assumed that grievances were rarely responded to, or maybe they really didn't think about it. Their focus still remained fixed on convincing their opponents that they had political power, and other matters were secondary. When the assistant manager made the rounds of the tenants, he discovered that a substantial number of the listed complaints had already been answered. The list even included a tenant who had moved from public housing a month earlier. After seeing the report and reflecting on the behavior of the organizers, O'Rourke concluded that they were neither trustworthy nor responsible, and he discontinued the negotiations.

NAC was convinced that turning over the list of tenants to the Housing Authority was a major blunder. Even though they told O'Rourke that the list of strikers was only a partial one, they assumed that he did not believe them. In other words, the organizers assumed that negotiations were broken off because O'Rourke discovered that they were, in fact, without substantial power. Two months later, they decided to end the strike. The mayoralty election was over, and the risk of eviction was great. The tenants insisted that their money be returned, and the organizers themselves were tired of the strike that had begun fourteen months earlier. George notified the Housing Authority that the strike had ended and the rent money was returned to the tenants. They refused to transfer the funds directly to the Housing Authority, which would have been a formal admission of defeat.

II

We have seen how objective conditions, coupled with factors internal to the character of NAC, favored a political style based upon creating an illusion of power. Such factors as the dearth of other tenant organizations, the alienated character of the tenant population in Rogers Point, and NAC's own scant resources provided a narrow field in which to operate effectively. The social attitudes and political beliefs of NAC also conspired to severely restrict its strategic options. The organization was left politically isolated and relatively powerless. Attempting to bluff the establishment through creating an illusion of power thus became a relatively practical alternative for NAC.

However, NAC's attempt to generate certain illusions was motivated by more than a sense of political expediency. The persistent faith and ardent commitment shown by the organizers, who employed tactical ruses despite their clear lack of success, suggests that other factors were involved. Three major factors, each to be considered in turn, seemed crucial: the gratification derived from bluffing the establishment; the tendency to systematically overestimate their own abilities and powers; and the tendency to underestimate the abilities of the establishment, particularly the Housing Authority.

Certainly, behavior can be expressive and goal-directed at the same time. But throughout the strike, there were numerous instances in which the organizers behaved as if their goals were secondary or irrelevant. For example, in court they actually giggled a good deal in self-appreciation of their tactics to convince the Housing Authority of their influence and power. These inappropriate celebrations actually undermined their effectiveness. The organizers simply did not realize what kind of an impression they were creating.

There seemed to be something about the process of attempting to bluff their opponents that offered its own rewards. The discussions that frequently took place after their encounters with the establishment suggested that a euphoric sense of superiority was the major prize. A few of these meetings that I attended took on the character of little victory celebrations; one of the organizers would pick up beer and potato chips, and they would sit around for a while, recapturing and boasting about their experience.

The pursuit of other psychic gains also appreciably influenced their political behavior. Asserting their autonomy, as suggested in their emphasis on "doing things their way," was important enough to override practical aims. This is why they were able to view their abrupt termination of the Rogers Point meeting with the Housing Authority as cause for celebration. The considerable importance of feeling and asserting their independence, particularly against Caucasians, was indirectly revealed in the following incident. A white acquaintance told Curtis that he would like to go along with him to a meeting that evening of community groups in the Granada area. Curtis quickly responded, "It's not necessary. I can handle things myself." His remark was inappropriate because he wasn't being offered any assistance. This incident, and others like it, showed his sensitivity to even small and indirect encroachments upon autonomy.

Whether showing their autonomy, asserting their presumed superiority, or in other ways feeding their self-esteem, the gratifications they derived frequently took precedence over their political objectives. Yet they generally justified their behavior in terms of its practical merits, that is, in terms of its contribution toward achieving long-range goals. By standing up to the establishment on their own terms, the organizers felt they were flexing their political muscles, and they thought that this, in turn, would favorably influence their odds for achieving victory. A gain that they did not speak about but which was immensely important was the "sense of being alive" that these encounters provided. The considerable joy these experiences appeared to induce apparently predisposed them toward a favorable evaluation of the political effectiveness of their behavior. In other words, the heavy emotional investment that these psychic gains entailed created a strong incentive to interpret them as effective political tools. It created a fertile ground in which to overestimate their own power and underestimate the abilities of the establishment.

Though these gratifications encouraged the organizers to bluff the etablishment, their creating an illusion of power also reflected a conviction of their own invincibility. For example, even toward the end of the strike, they still believed in their abilities to convince the Housing Authority that they had a substantial following; in fact, they even thought there was reasonable substance to their exaggerations. This virtually unshakable faith in their own abilities and strength was related to their conception of power. They treated power not as an activity but as a possession, something that belonged to them. In the context of the rent strike, to conceive of power as an activity would have implied seeing themselves as agents who were mobilizing resources to extract concessions from an opponent, namely the Housing Authority. In other words, they would have seen themselves as using power to accomplish certain tasks.

But by acting as if power is primarily a highly valued possession, a thing worth having and preserving rather than using, they tended to make it an end rather than a means. In treating it essentially as a possession, there is little more one can do than admire it, check to make sure that it is in his possession, and prevent others from taking it away. This is how the organizers, particularly Curtis, treated and interpreted power. Other persons and experiences became means to reassure themselves that they possessed power. Opponents became defined, to a large extent, not as objects capable of yielding concessions but as persons or institutions who would attempt to rob them of what they possessed. Take the example of the white acquaintance whom Curtis rebuked for asking permission to attend a meeting. Curtis, in effect, perceived this request essentially as an attempted robbery, which was aimed to challenge or "take away" his powers to handle his own political affairs. Curtis scored points, in his view, because he kept his possession intact. Clearly, the criteria for failure or success were structured by this conception of power as a possession.

But what, precisely, were the cues that convinced Curtis and the others that they had power? Their interpretation of power was largely related to their posture toward authority. If they emerged from real or imagined confrontations with authority by standing firm on their demands, then they demonstrated to their own satisfaction that they possessed power. In other words, they had left the bargaining table without having given anything up.

But although this politics of style did reap victories over the Mexican leadership of the Granada poverty program, it did not gain real concessions from the Housing Authority. The gains they made were symbolic ones, achieved in two ways: first, they fantasized encounters with the Housing Authority which resulted in its destruction and subjugation; and second, in actual encounters with the Housing Authority they achieved symbolic victories.

During the many months of the rent strike, the organizers engaged in a great deal of talk around the office about what to do about the Housing Authority. Various ideas were repeatedly suggested but never passed the discussion stage. "Yep, it's getting time for a couple hundred of us to sit in and make a ruckus downtown," was one strategy that was almost regularly put forth. Curtis was more fertile and effusive than the others. He threatened to bring a dozen rats to the commission meeting and "let 'em loose." Eddie Daniels issued the most daring threat. Referring to the top black administrator at the Housing Authority, he said, "You know, we're going to put Edwards on the list. If these guys don't come across, they're not going to see the light of day."

The "list," of course, was presumably made up of black men to be assassinated.

All of the organizers participated in fantasizing how they would humiliate, subjugate, or altogether destroy the Housing Authority. They seemed, on occasion, to be well aware that they were only engaging in idle bull sessions. But there were also many occasions when they appeared quite convinced that some or all of these proposals would be actually carried out. The nature of the gratification they derived from these speculations was particularly important. It really made them feel exceedingly courageous. This was particularly characteristic of Curtis, who almost convinced me that he might physically abuse the executive director of the Housing Authority.

However, when they actually confronted establishment spokesmen, these fantasies were inadequate to sustain their image of themselves as courageous or powerful. Though the organizers took their own boasts quite seriously, they really had no intention of harming officials of the Housing Authority or carrying out any of their other threats. They had apparently tended to shift the criteria of success toward the achievement of symbolic rather than instrumental victories when confronting the establishment. But whether fantasizing about or actually confronting their opponents, their criteria rested mainly upon the ability to "stand up to the Man" and "put him in his place."

Their orientation toward power, with its attendant emphasis upon reaffirming their "possession," tended to undermine an instrumental perspective, one which would evaluate achievements in terms of changing the practices of the Housing Authority. At the meeting back in their office after breaking off negotiations with the Housing Authority, their victory celebration noticeably excluded any discussion about how they might have used the leverage that such a public meeting offered to gain support for their demands. In this instance their symbolic victory undermined their stated goal of achieving reforms, because they closed the meeting before even presenting their grievances. Had they employed instrumental criteria for evaluating their power, they would not have been engaging in a victory celebration afterward.

In short, perceiving power as a possession caused them to redefine the rules for testing their strength, which in turn encouraged them to overestimate themselves. The exaggeration of their powers was reflected, first, in the assumption that they could employ daring ruses without risking discovery, and second, in the belief that the illusion of power they were attempting to foster could not be illusory in fact.

The blindness of not properly appreciating the ability of the Housing Authority to detect their ruses reflected, in part, their vision of how organizations and their administrators operated. Specifically, they did not understand how a bureaucracy operates, they misread the style and demeanor of Housing Authority officials, and they misjudged the types of pressures that made the Housing Authority vulnerable. Their failure to grasp the nature of bureaucratic organization, with its complex system of record-keeping, has been mentioned earlier. They really did not understand how an accounting system, made up of machines and clerks, provided an intelligence apparatus for administrators.

What did exist for them were flesh and blood individuals, particularly the Housing Authority's major executives with whom they had established personal contact. Whether or not they thought particular individuals could be bluffed would depend to a great extent upon how they evaluated their abilities. In their view, the Housing Authority administrators were very short on intelligence. They knew that the top posts were political appointments, and argued that ability was therefore an irrelevant consideration. What they failed to consider was that even if their evaluation was accurate, these executives were still supported by an elaborate, though not conspicuous, system of intelligence which kept them informed.

As evidence that their strategy was effective, they saw O'Rourke's affable, friendly manner as proof that he recognized the "awesome" powers of NAC. Just as they believed that their own strength was reflected in their demeanor, so they thought that the weakness of the Housing Authority administrators was revealed in theirs. In our discussion of NAC's battles with the Mexican administration of the Granada poverty program, we noted how they interpreted the executive director's style similarly. Lopez was affable and ingratiating, which to them was a sign of weakness. With regard to the Housing Authority administrators, NAC began to learn that a mild manner did not necessarily yield concessions, and they even became somewhat resentful of this even-tempered style, which in fact often characterizes the behavior of executives in public agencies. Still, the organizers never wholly surrendered the illusion that the agreeable manner of these administrators would be followed by some concessions.

Unlike his predecessor, O'Rourke made it his policy to meet with tenant groups. In fact, he prided himself on being in contact with the poor and concerned with their problems. At meetings with public officials and influential citizens, he projected himself as an administrator who really cared about tenants. But the organizers, who were accustomed to employing "battle rhetoric" in their dealings with opponents, had difficulty understanding the meaning of this style. They themselves would sound placating only if on the verge of defeat, and they incorrectly assumed that this principle applied to establishment bureaucrats.

The organizers both misunderstood and underestimated the technical abilities and political ingenuity of the establishment, just as they tended to overestimate their own political strength. Of course, often the relative strength or weakness of a political contender can only be crudely estimated, and is in itself variable. From other confrontations between City Hall and community groups, there was certainly evidence that the establishment could be forced to make important concessions to the poor.

The organizers drew a certain amount of courage from the fact that community groups won control of the poverty program. Every black leader in Presentation City understood that minority control of the poverty program was won, in part, through militant threats of massive disruptive tactics. Despite the mayor's declarations that he would never relinquish control of the program, he did finally acquiesce. The representatives of the poor did a considerable amount of political planning and made many friends, even within the establishment. Most important, the federal government refused to release funds until a consensus was reached in the City. This gave virtually any recalcitrant organization some leverage to stall or sabotage the program.

But NAC tended to ignore these features of the political battle when considering how the poor succeeded. They tended to be more impressed with the great fanfare that some of the black leaders created. What they typically harped on were those aspects of the political struggle that were the noisiest and most bombastic. They remembered the shouting, name calling, and threats, which they believed, in the final analysis, had won the war for the poor. In short, the organizers tended to misinterpret and recreate experience to conform to a political style largely oriented toward demeanor, and this provided fertile ground for developing political strategies based upon creating an illusion of power. Unfortunately, for the organizers and the tenants, their orientation deflected them from the political goals of the strike.

CHAPTER FIVE

NAC AND
THE LAWYERS

THE MILITANT black nationalist spirit that guided the politics of NAC made white lawyers most unlikely allies in their effort to sustain and win the rent strike. The color white was beyond the pale, and dealing with these "professional types," as they were pejoratively called by the organizers, posed two great risks. First, professionals were assumed to be politically conservative, which made them untrustworthy and even dangerous. Second, their training and status were believed to foster arrogance, which in turn would cause them to dictate terms to their clients rather than respond to their wishes and needs. The organizers therefore believed that suspicion was a reasonable posture toward lawyers, and surveillance of their activities was regarded as necessary conduct. Most important, the organizers, not the lawyers, must "call the shots."

Ordinarily, lawyers refuse to represent clients who treat them with distrust, challenge their professional competence, and interfere with their efforts to operate in the manner they think best. Dealing with political militants may often pose these problems for lawyers. The decidedly conflicting styles of militant organizers and most lawyers could make a working relationship between them tenuous, short-lived, or even impossible.

However, unusual circumstances brought about and

sustained a relationship, however tenuous and unstable, between a group of liberal lawyers and NAC. The organizers
felt compelled to obtain legal assistance because they feared
the collapse of the rent strike. About two months after it
was organized, tenants were served notices by the Housing
Authority that unless they met their rent payments, eviction
proceedings would be brought against them. The striking
tenants panicked, and the organizers, who had no previous
experience organizing rent strikes, were in a turmoil. Jerry
Cook busily assured the tenants who wanted to defect that
there was nothing to fear. The other organizers, meanwhile,
immediately contacted the neighborhood OEO legal service
office, which provided free legal assistance to the poor.

The peculiar history and consequent structure of this
organization made it extremely difficult for it to refuse service to any client, no matter how undesirable he might seem
to the lawyers. The City's Economic Opportunity Council,
rather than the Presentation City Bar Association, approved
the funding of this organization because community leaders
were assured that it would be responsive to neighborhood
needs and issues. To incorporate this principle into its structure, the Presentation City Legal Service Association (The
Association) promised that the majority of the Board of
Directors would be recruited from the poverty target areas.

Further, the organization was publicly committed to
the policy of using its resources to bring about social and
economic changes in poor communities. In pursuit of this
goal, it sought to represent organizational as well as individual clients. The lawyers believed that by advocating the
claims raised by organizations, they would be more likely to
confront the causes of poverty. So unlike the local bar association's Legal Aid Society, which was serving only individual clients, The Association took on this larger commitment
—which became, from the point of view of the poverty

neighborhoods, an expectation. For the organization to have offended clients, then, particularly organizational ones, meant risking being accused of betraying the poor.

The legal problems of the organizers and the social commitments of The Association, then, provided the framework that sustained a most unlikely alliance. The character of this alliance unfolded during three successive phases of the partners' relationship; first, the initial meetings between them, when legal strategies were planned; second, the trials of the tenants; and third, the events related to the planning and conducting of negotiations with the Housing Authority.

II

The initial encounters between the lawyers and the organizers moved rapidly from conventional professional-client meetings to near disaster. After amicably agreeing with a proposed plan of action put forth by Stanley Berke, the Chief Counsel of the Granada neighborhood office of the Association, the organizers angrily withdrew their prior approval.

Stanley, a lawyer in his mid-thirties, had never before served poor black clients and had no prior personal contacts with militants. But being quite liberal politically, he was pleased with the prospect of defending and advocating the interests of public housing tenants. In the first few meetings with the organizers, Stanley advised them of their legal status and advanced a proposal that he believed was appropriate to their situation. In brief, he explained that state law offered no sanctuaries for rent strikers. Legal precedent had been established that the obligation of tenants to pay rent was not mitigated by a failure or even refusal of a landlord to maintain his premises. To argue in court that housing was substandard offered no defense for rent delinquent tenants. In the municipal courts of Presentation City, the judges had consistently favored the landlord against tenants on the issue of rent delinquency; in this, the judges simply adhered to the letter and intent of the law.

In view of the poor legal prognosis for the tenants, Stanley proposed an agreement whereby NAC would put its money in trust to a third party if the Housing Authority would drop its eviction proceedings against the tenants and indicate its willingness to negotiate. Stanley claimed that there would be two important advantages to creating a trust fund. First, NAC could avoid possible criminal charges for the illegal possession of funds. Second, The Association was willing to prepare a separate suit against the Housing Authority to legally compel it to properly maintain its projects. This suit would also seek to guarantee that the tenants could continue to withhold their rent without the danger of eviction, at least until the case was decided by the courts. According to Stanley, a federal court would be most unlikely to agree to this stipulation if the rent money collected was still being hidden in an unknown location.

The organizers consented to this proposal on condition that the Housing Authority drop eviction proceedings and begin to negotiate. At the moment, this seemed to the organizers to be an ideal approach for continuing the strike with a minimum of risk to themselves and the tenants. Stanley then contacted the Housing Authority and, through its attorneys, succeeded in convincing it to accept the plan. To the Housing Authority, Stanley's proposal had certain distinct advantages. First, the rent money would be protected. Second, the Housing Authority, whose new executive director was anxious to project a progressive image, would enjoy an opportunity to show its sincerity and interest in the project tenants. The new executive director had publicly acknowledged that much was wrong with public housing, and he was seeking means to work with tenants to improve conditions.

However, when the chief counsel informed the organizers of what he believed was good news, they had apparently changed their minds. Curtis argued that surrendering control over the collected rent would strip NAC of an important weapon. Further, putting the money in trust would imply that they were untrustworthy, which was an insult. They spoke with considerable anger. Curtis accused Stanley of betraying both the tenants and the organizers. They wondered whether The Association was conspiring with the Housing Authority. As Curtis put it, "They think the Housing Authority is their client, not us." The organizers then demanded that the tenants be represented in court.

Actually, their turnabout was quite understandable. Their initial panic had subsided. Jerry had been able to quiet the tenants and prevent defections from the strike. They also reminded themselves that the Housing Authority had not been evicting and would be unlikely to do so in the near future. Thus the proposal's initial luster seemed to become tarnished after careful consideration.

The organizers' initial acquiescence and later anger seemed to be connected. These militant, nationalist organizers sought, in a state of panic, not only the advice and assistance of white professional lawyers, but they did so with appreciable humility. At the early meetings, they raised none of the questions and concerns that were to disturb them later on. Instead, they listened carefully, and restricted their interventions almost exclusively to requests for clarification. From a lawyer's perspective, Curtis and the others were behaving as reasonable clients in trouble.

But these organizers were no ordinary clients. Frightened by the impending collapse of the strike, they had momentarily dropped their guard. Behaving as if almost totally dependent upon the mercy of a white lawyer was, in fact, a posture quite alien to their political and personal self-image. Their acquiescent stance must have later embarrassed and frightened them. Reacting against this unguarded exposure, they recoiled by rejecting Stanley's proposal with abruptness and anger. Rage became the vehicle for recapturing self-esteem.

In explaining themselves, the organizers claimed that they were "pissed off" after realizing that "that crud took us in." This suggests that the anxiety stirred up by almost "selling out" partly explained their reaction. But the dependency issues were certainly important. On other occasions throughout the strike, their abrupt transition from an acquiescent posture to adamant resistance, whether expressed in lashing out or withdrawing, could be predicted. On each occasion, they had an explanation for their change of mind. Of course, there is nothing idiosyncratic about reevaluating decisions and behavior, and consequently in responding with some anxiety. Especially notable, though, in this instance as well as in others, was the extreme variance of their behavior. First, they would display complete obedience, then they would respond with anger or withdrawal. We shall see later how this pattern of behavior operates in other situations.

Stanley felt confused, angry, and injured. He had to embarrass himself by reneging on the agreement arrived at with the attorney for the Housing Authority, who began to ask whether The Association really represented the tenant union. The chief counsel suspected that the organizers were either mentally deranged or had ulterior political motives. He was particularly suspicious of Curtis, and regarded him as mainly responsible for the tensions that developed.

Further fueling the tensions was the refusal of the organizers to permit any Association attorney to meet privately with any of the striking tenants. During the same period, a recent law school graduate, Morris Rosen, was assigned to spent part of his time becoming acquainted with the organizers and the tenants. Stanley believed that major legal issues could emerge from Rogers Point, so he was willing to allow a staff member to work closely with this community. The organizers responded favorably to The Association's interest, but Morris was warned that no tenants could be interviewed by him without the presence of an organizer.

Throughout the strike, NAC considered Rogers Point its exclusive turf, and all visitors to the community were accompanied by guides—namely, one of the organizers. Moreover, according to NAC, the organizers rather than the tenants were the client. Stanley believed, on the other hand, that the tenants were ultimately the clients, and free access to them was required in order to serve them fully. The refusal of NAC to cooperate on this issue was extremely irritating to the lawyers. They believed that this policy impeded their professional work, and they found being distrusted very distasteful.

Unsure how to proceed with NAC, Stanley requested a meeting with both the chief counsels from the other poverty target area law offices and The Association's executive director, who was situated in the main office. Each chief counsel presided over policy issues in his own community. But discussions, and often debates, among themselves provided an opportunity to develop clarity and perspective. Stanley, who was angry with the organizers but sympathetic to the tenants, was ambivalent about retaining the case. Other staff members who attended had their own distinct opinions, which were, interestingly enough, divided along racial lines.

The two black chief counsels opted for an ultimatum to the organizers that unless the lawyers were permitted to "run the show," NAC would be dropped. They stressed the issue of professional integrity, claiming that no client should ever be permitted to undermine it. Their indignation was great. Stanley found both their anger and their proposed resolution to the crisis disturbing. He considered his own judgment better than that of the organizers, which was a posture that frequently triggered tension between the organizers and The Association. However, watching these angry black lawyers, Stanley reacted adversely to the image of a self-righteous attorney waving a finger at a client. The director, who was also Caucasian, urged, on the other hand, a policy of understanding and cooperation with NAC. He stated: "One thing that distinguishes us from the legal aid society is that we want to establish a relationship with the community. We've got to listen to the organizers. Sure, they might be crazy and exasperating. But they're our client."

Both the director's advice and his own adverse reaction to the stance of the black lawyers swayed Stanley toward making an effort to work with NAC. He decided that The Association would represent the tenants in court even though the chances of winning these cases were poor. The organization would also pay court filing fees, which were required of tenants who answered summonses to appear in court. Furthermore, specialist lawyers in the main office would prepare a federal suit against the Housing Authority on behalf of NAC and the tenants in the Rogers Point projects.

These decisions were communicated to the organizers, who interpreted them as a direct response to their hard line. It was clear that the organizers reveled in the belief that they were intimidating The Association. For example, they suspected, with some accuracy, that the lawyers would informally arrange crisis meetings in response to disturbances triggered by NAC. When I visited NAC's office after one incident, Curtis asked in his characteristically sardonic style, "Tell me, Harry, did they call another one of their meetings yesterday?" The lawyers, however, saw no subservience in their decision to represent and cooperate with NAC.

In addition to professional considerations, organizational factors imposed limits upon the capacity of The Association to bend to NAC's will. A serious conflict arose when NAC demanded that only one lawyer be assigned to represent all their tenants. At his own office, Stanley himself was occupied with administrative and supervisorial tasks; Morris, a recent law school graduate, could not practice until he received the results of his bar examination; another lawyer, who was Spanish-speaking, was needed to handle the large number of neighborhood Latin American clients; and the only other lawyer at the office was occupied with other tasks.

Further, the chief counsels from the other offices could not be expected to sacrifice any of their attorneys. The Association was a free legal service program, and the neighborhood offices were swamped with clients, both organizations and individuals. To commit a lawyer full-time for an indefinite period when each office was already burdened with clients was considered both unwise and impractical. Nevertheless, the chief counsel and The Association's director agreed to release lawyers in their offices to handle several cases. Thus different lawyers would be responsible for different tenants, but Stanley would supervise them and would continue to deal directly with the organizers, who could express their concerns directly to him.

The Association believed that it had found a reasonable arrangement for handling the public housing cases, and also thought that its allocation of resources to NAC was generous, particularly in view of the relatively slim chances of winning in court. NAC, understandably, took a quite different view. The organizers believed that the assignment of several lawyers rather than a single one to defend the tenants against evictions would necessarily dilute the quality of service. In their view, sincerity and interest on the part of The Association would have cut through bureaucratic impediments. According to the organizers, they were being "sold out."

A related issue that generated tensions arose over the scheduling of court cases. The organizers demanded that only one trial be held on a given day. The Association rejected this request because it would deplete its already meager resources. NAC's rationale was a political one. The organizers believed that in the long run the tenants would win not through litigation but by building a political organization. The Association had already pointed out the likelihood of losing in court. The organizers reasoned that stringing out the cases over an extended period would provide NAC with a greater opportunity to build an organization, and thus to become a more formidable political opponent, regardless of the results in court.

Though the lawyers were mainly oriented toward seeking legal and administrative solutions rather than political ones, the decision on how to represent the tenants was essentially based upon the organization's limited resources. The organizers were reminded that just as they had obligations other than the rent strike, The Association also had other commitments to honor, including the representation of other organizations. This was unacceptable to the organizers; their propensity of considering other groups in the City as "finks" convinced them that they deserved priority. In summing up NAC's response to The Association's explanation for its policy, George said, "that's bullshit." He explained NAC's position as follows: "Harry, whose side are they on, ours or the Housing Authority? They say they want to help us. Then why don't they act that way? When you ask them to do something, they give you that fucking legal talk. That's bullshit in my language."

The organizers not only believed that they were getting the short end of the stick; they also had an explanation. They were being victimized by a white establishment organization for being black militants. Not being in a position to rid itself of NAC, The Association was presumed to be resorting to devious means to encourage NAC to withdraw on its own. This feeling of being betrayed because they were militants was serious enough to cause them to freely inform other persons in the community that the interests of the tenants were being virtually abandoned by the lawyers. But being quite indignant, the organizers intended to make sure that The Association did not shirk its responsibilities. As George warned, "We're going to watch these lawyer finks damn closely." The distrust and anger that grew out of their encounters during this period set a tense tone for the second phase, when the tenants were brought to trial.

III

Whether inside or outside the courtroom, the behavior of the lawyers was strongly influenced by what they interpreted as the norms of their profession. The organizers, in turn, responded to their lawyers' behavior with greater suspicion and hostility toward The Association. Before trial proceedings, the lawyers, clients, and organizers would gather in the hallway outside the courtroom, where The Association attorneys and counsel for the Housing Authority would occasionally engage in amiable exchanges. To the various lawyers representing the tenants, this behavior in no way affected their ability to represent their clients effectively.

The organizers were aware, from other experiences in court, that this behavior of the attorneys was in line with usual practice; but observing their lawyers encounter the enemy in a relaxed and friendly manner nevertheless grated on them. Being familiar with this practice did not stop them from feeling that there was something terribly wrong with their lawyers' behavior. Throughout the trials, they continually mentioned that if the lawyers shared their indignation, they would at least ignore the opposition. "Look, Harry," Jerry claimed, "if somebody is fucking me, I don't sweet mouth them like those guys do. Do you see any of us asking those pricks how they feel today?"

These professionally sanctioned friendly conversations between lawyers on opposing sides of a case also created an atmosphere of distrust. The organizers suspected that confiding in their lawyers carried with it the danger of being betrayed.

Jerry: We can't tell them everything. They'll stool on us.

Me: C'mon, Jerry. That's carrying things pretty far. You got these lawyers wrong.

Jerry: You're missing the point, Harry. When you're friendly with a guy, you don't watch what you say. It's human nature. Would you tell something important to a guy who's friendly to your enemy?

The organizers never brought these concerns to the attention of the lawyers. They probably assumed that nothing would change, which was most likely an accurate assessment, for many of the Association's lawyers, while doing their job in the courtroom, had great difficulty understanding the point of view of the tenants.

The behavior of The Association's legal staff also generated animosity and suspicion within the courtroom. Being lawyers, their legal strategy was primarily directed toward winning their cases. To the disappointment of the organizers, this required that technical rather than moral issues be stressed, particularly since the cases were being argued before a judge, not a jury. As we have noted, the emotionally heavy issue of deteriorated housing conditions was not a relevant defense for the refusal to pay rent. Legally, a landlord's failure to maintain premises does not relieve tenants of their financial responsibility.

Instead, the cogent legal issue was how the Housing Authority delivered its three-day notices, which ordered tenants to meet their rent payments or be subject to eviction proceedings. The law required that these notices be delivered in person. The Housing Authority claimed to have met this legal requirement, but the tenants maintained that the notices had been slipped under the door. The strategy adopted by Stanley in consultation with the other lawyers was to attempt to prove that these notices were illegally served. The reason for pursuing this tack was explained to the organizers. They were also informed that the lawyers would be allowed to raise the issue of poor housing conditions in court, but that this issue would be elaborated and more urgently stressed in the federal suit against the Housing Authority; it was explained that this could not be the main basis for pursuing the defense of the tenants.

The political interests of the organizers led them to protest this approach. It seemed a passionless tactic and conflicted with their desire to impress the tenants, many of whom were wavering about remaining on strike, with a forceful and dramatic defense. They were also anxious to impress the tenants with their ability to obtain excellent lawyers. In this regard, even though the organizers frequently denounced The Association, they never expressed their objections to the tenants. Most important, they believed that the Housing Authority should be exposed and humiliated in court. Before trial they often told the lawyers to "give 'em hell" and "put 'em in their place." Tension between the organizers and The Association naturally increased. The legal stress on a technical defense of the tenants fed the organizers' suspicion that they were being "sold out."

During the trials, which spanned a six-month period, eight lawyers represented sixteen tenants. Most of them followed instructions, which meant that they pressed the technical defense while attempting when possible to introduce into testimony tenant complaints against the Housing Authority. The lawyers differed in the ways they mixed these two tactics. The evaluation made of each lawyer by the organizers varied accordingly. Lawyers who seemed to stress the technical defense at the presumed expense of the moral issues were often severely criticized; they would be chided for their misdeeds, and Stanley or other Association administrators would soon be confronted with their complaints. The lawyers and administrators were both confused and angry, and expressed their feelings to each other quite freely. During such crises they even considered severing ties with NAC. But they nevertheless assumed an air of professional detachment when encountering the organizers, and attempted to explain to them that they were doing their best.

The lawyers and the NAC obviously had different standards for evaluating legal competence. Not having legal background and training, the NAC organizers tended to be insensitive to the requirements of the court. They were most interested in courtroom style, which they related to the norms of street life. If a lawyer projected himself as "fighting mad," he proved himself; appearing to be on the right side was basically their measure of a lawyer's competence in the courtroom. Jerry Cook described what he thought a good lawyer would do: "You don't sit there. You keep getting up and objecting. You wear 'em down until they've had it. Any of us could do better than most of those guys, and none of us went to law school."

This conception of an ideal lawyer as one who assumes a noticeably aggressive stance influenced the organizers' behavior in the courtroom. During the trials they would explain with much gusto to those sitting near them how each lawyer should be performing. In fact, I was frequently asked to pass on their advice to the various lawyers while the trials were actually in progress. The advice usually concerned how the attorney could make more frequent and effective interventions in the case.

The lawyers, on the other hand, stressed criteria for legal competence that seemed uninspiring to the organizers. The lawyers believed that a competent attorney who argues before only a judge in the courtroom emphasizes legal rather than moral argument. Furthermore, he should strive for an economy of style: he should object or intervene only according to a criterion of legal relevance, and not appreciably overstate his case. In these eviction proceedings, the legal basis was relatively restricted, and this frustrated the organizers. Though The Association administrators vaguely understood this gap in perception, they were noticeably irritated by the inability of the organizers to appreciate their efforts.

To the organizers, competence and sincerity were virtually identical. The lawyers who pressed hard were assumed to be both competent and concerned. The lawyers themselves did not equate these attributes, but they did believe that the more sincere and dedicated lawyers would naturally concentrate upon scoring legal points rather than "clowning." Certainly, they believed that flair and style could add to a lawyer's ability to win cases, but they also felt that when he "horses around," he and his clients are in trouble.

Significantly, the lawyer who stressed the technical issues most strongly was generally evaluated by the other lawyers as being extremely devoted. The lawyer who "put on a big show" for the organizers, according to Stanley, was judged by several Association employees to be relatively indifferent to his clients. These assessments were exactly opposite to those made by the organizers, which partially explains the Association's exasperation and NAC's discontent.

When lawyer Peter Thorne restricted his defense to the technical issues involved, the organizers became enraged. He seemed to them too detached and unemotional. They believed that he really didn't "give a hoot." Curtis remarked angrily immediately after the trial, "The Association should be flushed down the sewer." When they expressed their indignation to Peter, he patiently tried to explain his legal strategy, but they were most unsympathetic. They had branded him as insincere because of his failure to adopt a moral stance in court. The lawyers on the other hand, considered him highly committed. In fact, Peter was an active member of the left-wing National Lawyers Guild, and later on he resigned from The Association to join a left-wing law firm. His political orientation actually made him very interested in serving clients like NAC.

The Association staff was offended by the charges made against Peter. He voluntarily worked longer hours than most of the attorneys, and seemed to other staff members to be unusually patient with even the most difficult clients. That Peter handled a case without fanfare explained to the lawyers why he was regarded as lethargic by the organizers, but they saw his style as evidence of his integrity.

The contrasting response of NAC and The Association

to another lawyer, Jules Cohen, who conducted one trial with enormous vitality and involvement, provided another example of their very different criteria for evaluating legal competence. Jules continuously objected to the Housing Authority's line of questioning and otherwise fully involved himself in the trial proceedings. In brief, he gave the kind of performance that the organizers very much wanted to see. All of them were elated. Curtis shook his hand and congratulated him warmly and at length.

The organizers would undoubtedly have been surprised at Jules' own attitude toward the trial experience. Upon returning to the office, he lightheartedly remarked, "They wanted a show, so I gave them one. But what bullshit this is; it comes to nothing." To a layman, he undoubtedly performed impressively, but, according to staff members who worked in his office, he seemed to be relatively uninvolved in his work. In fact, he spent a considerable amount of time doing legal work which was irrelevant to the goals and interests of The Association.

Neither the organizers nor The Association believed that they were understood by the other. Stanley, who was irritated by the organizers' favorable response to Jules, said: "You know, they wouldn't know a good lawyer if they saw one. All Jules was doing was giving them a good show, and they go wild." The organizers saw this differently. Curtis said: "We're not expecting miracles. We know these cases are difficult to win. But we want the lawyers to try. Jules Cohen tried. That's all we expect."

Only once were the organizers wholly satisfied with a technical defense, and this occasion proved to be most revealing. With only a few cases left for The Association to represent, Morris, who had earlier been assigned by Stanley to work in Rogers Point, received his license to practice law. Taking one of the few remaining cases, he became the only attorney to score a legal victory. Fortunately for Morris, there were unusual facts in this case. The defendent who testified was the only tenant brought to trial who was currently living with her husband in the projects. According to a signed statement by a Housing Authority representative, the three-day notice was delivered to the male head of the household. Morris at once told the court that the husband was a full-time employee, and argued that since the notices were delivered during regular working hours, he could not have received it personally. The judge dismissed the case.

The organizers, of course, were jubilant. Finally a lawyer had won one of their cases. Though no other attorney had a case with similar circumstances, Morris' victory was not regarded as coincidental by the organizers. On the contrary, in a discussion later at their office, Morris' success was viewed as evidence that the other cases had been needlessly lost, and that the disinterest and lack of ability of the other lawyers accounted for their failure to win. It was particularly significant that the organizers related his success to his earlier contact with the Rogers Point community. As Jerry said: "I knew Morris wouldn't let us down. When this thing got started, he came around here and got to know us and the tenants. He got to know our problems. Let's face it. That's why Morris won. And he would have won a hell of a lot more."

There was no logical connection between Morris' legal victory and his contact with the community, since the case did not depend on any knowledge of housing conditions there. But to the organizers, there was a twofold relationship. First, they believed that contact with the community created concern for their problems, which in turn generated a will to win. Second, community contact was assumed to have relevant educational value, which instilled competence that enhanced the ability of the lawyer to win his case.

The readiness to believe that Morris' winning the case

was related to contact with the community was based largely upon how the organizers viewed themselves and what they thought about the legal profession. For one thing, they were prone to self-flattery. Although they considered themselves exceedingly shrewd, they were remarkably gullible about accepting ideas that would cast them in a desirable light. They thought that somehow their experience and ideas would rub off upon those who came into contact with them. White professionals certainly have a great deal to learn from indigenous groups, but the organizers were unjustifiably predisposed to take credit for the accomplishments of others who had associated with them.

Nor did the organizers really appreciate the considerable skill required for professional work. Such personal attributes as sincerity would take on an exaggerated significance for them. Since Morris was believed to be highly motivated, they could readily believe that this went a long way toward explaining why he had won the case. And further, they assumed that he was sincere because of his frequent appearances in their community. Here again, while making such a connection seems plausible, there was really no evidence that Morris was appreciably more concerned with their interests than the other lawyers.

In any case, there is a great deal more to being an effective lawyer than sincerity or competence derived from grass roots contact. A major reason that the organizers did not fully appreciate this was their tendency to perceive differences in occupations in essentially quantitative terms. They seemed to think that occupations differed from one another mainly in degree of difficulty rather than being qualitatively distinct. They took this view particularly toward jobs that involved talk. Though jobs requiring verbal skills may in fact have little else in common, they assumed that there was very little that differentiated them.

Jerry Cook, for example, considered himself a "great bullshitter," as proven by his abilty to keep the tenants on strike. He assumed that if he were magically bestowed with a law degree, he would with hardly any training be an excellent lawyer. That was why he and the other organizers felt competent to advise the lawyers on legal matters in court. One aspect of this perspective, at least with regard to the belief that they were in effect lawyers without licenses, was the emphasis upon demeanor and performance when evaluating competence. In their evaluation of Morris Rosen, they believed that the competence he developed through contact with the Rogers Point community was readily transferable to the courtroom because the different skill requirements in each setting were thought to be essentially a matter of extent rather than of kind.

Their satisfaction with both Morris and Jules did not reduce tensions between the organizers and The Association. On the contrary, the successful handling of the trials by these two lawyers precipitated crisis situations. In both instances, the organizers complained to Association administrators that the superior representation these attorneys offered demonstrated the lack of interest and incompetence of the other lawyers. Even more important, they saw the assignment of these presumably poorly qualified lawyers as clear evidence of the conservative, establishment-oriented policies of The Association. In short, NAC believed it was receiving low priority because of its political militancy.

It was immediately after Jules Cohen impressed the organizers in court that they first charged that he was the only satisfactory lawyer assigned to them. This was surprising, because they had already made comments indicating approval of how several lawyers had conducted their trials. The attorneys had generally stressed a technical defense, but they also made efforts to inject the issue of deteriorated housing. Though the organizers did not wholly approve of their court presentations, there was reason for them to express some satisfaction. When they later denied that any of them were worthwhile, they did not seem to be insincere; rather they appeared to have changed their minds.

From their perspective, the other lawyers paled in comparison to Jules, no matter what they had previously believed about them. Further, their deep distrust for this white, middle-class organization appeared too basic to maintain stable working relationships with its white lawyers. The antagonism toward The Association—exacerbated, ironically, by their favorable response to Jules—is as an excellent example of how precarious the coalition between these two organizations was. This instance also reveals a marked tendency to interpret even favorable events as signs of betrayal.

Though NAC's deep sense of distrust for The Association generated a great deal of tension between them, this by no means exhausted the factors that created estrangement. Impressed as they were with Jules' performance, the organizers resisted his efforts to gain their cooperation in winning cases. Jules, who was scheduled to represent other tenants, contrived a legal strategy that required one or two witnesses who lived in the projects. He proposed to the organizers that they bring them along for the next trial. His proposed tactic, which was aimed at "exposing" the Housing Authority, was eagerly welcomed by the organizers. As in their earlier meetings with Stanley Berke, Curtis and the other organizers seemed unusually attentive and approving; speaking for the organizers, Curtis assured Jules of NAC's cooperation.

However, to Jules' disappointment, the organizers not only failed to bring witnesses but, without even notifying The Association in advance, they and the defendants did not appear at all. Jules embarrassingly invented excuses before the judge, and obtained a trial postponement for the defendants. Afterward, Jules telephoned NAC's office, and Curtis, who answered, explained that "something had come up." Jules asked Curtis to bring witnesses for the next trial. But when the organizers appeared in court several days later, no witnesses accompanied them. Curtis said that they had been unable to locate anyone. In fact, they had not really tried. As I learned later, Curtis told Jerry not to bother because they had more important tasks to concern themselves with.

Both political and personal reasons must have deterred NAC from offering even minimal cooperation to Jules. Being black militants, cooperation with The Association and its predominantly white staff posed difficult problems for them. Undoubtedly, their battle stance against The Association was one mechanism that permitted, within the context of their philosophy, this alliance. By displaying antagonism, the organizers were able to avoid the implications of facing up to their cooperation with whites. Collaboration with Jules posed a challenge to this perspective. There were two problems with Jules' suggestion. First, it was his rather than theirs. Second, the character of the proposal made him the "brains" and them the "brawn." To have accepted his proposal would have, in effect, converted the organizers into his runners. Curtis frankly admitted that a major attraction of the black nationalist perspective was the avoiding of those dilemmas which made blacks the lackeys of white men, no matter what the presumed advantage for blacks.

This philosophy coincided with a deeply personal sensitivity about being cast in what appeared a subservient role. The organizers initially applauded Jules' plan because they respected the idea and thought highly of the lawyer who offered it. But these personal and political factors caused them to reverse their position later on. They handled this situation in a way that suggests a repetition of their familiar pattern of rebuke following swiftly upon the heels of acquiescence. In short, even Association practices that were regarded favorably by the organizers at first glance tended to fuel rather than extinguish tensions.

The Association lawyers were in a difficult situation. Despite their own irritation with NAC, they believed that it was important to establish relationships with such organizations. And as white citizens, they shared in the contemporary mood that being white meant that they really didn't understand blacks. So even when infuriated, Association spokesmen tried, though not always with the sensitivity demanded by the situation, to explain their own position and also to understand NAC's.

For the organizers, this conciliatory posture was often seen as an open invitation to take the offensive. Complementing the role of the lawyers, their indignant pose reflected the conviction that they were being misunderstood, and that an explanation for the conduct of the lawyers should be forthcoming. In other words, from the perspective of the organizers, the proper stance on the part of the lawyers should be one of deference and remorse. Since even efforts at achieving rapport triggered tension, the prognosis for the lawyers attaining more than a modicum of cooperation seemed poor. Their fear was given further support during phase three, which consisted of the planning and conducting of negotiations with the Housing Authority.

IV

The organizers were conscious of three sources of tension in their dealings with The Association. First, they believed that the lawyers were more politically conservative than themselves, which in their view explained the deliberate refusal of the organization to cooperate with them. Second, they resented the professional posture of the lawyers, with its attendant implications of superior competence; therefore they tended to rebuke proposals suggested by the lawyers, even when they were well-regarded. Third, they believed that whites did not understand black people, and this would necessarily corrupt the quality of services rendered. The issue of color was deeper than this argument suggests, but it was on this level of discourse that the antagonism to the whiteness of the lawyers was expressed. In short, political, professional, and racial issues were the decisive factors in creating almost impossible barriers between the organizers and The Association.

These factors were by no means equally weighted by the organizers. Perceiving themselves as primarily a political unit, they cited the political conservatism of the lawyers as the main barrier to cooperation. In virtually every crisis that developed between them they attributed to The Association ulterior political motives, which they expected from an establishment agency. Moreover, the political lenses through which they viewed The Association colored their interpretation of the other factors. What they considered the insolence of professionalism was also viewed as primarily a strategy of political co-optation. In other words, the advice that the lawyers were attempting to impose would presumably have diluted the militant character of NAC.

With regard to the race issue, they believed that whites as exploiters of blacks did not understand them because it was to their economic and political advantage to perceive issues only from their own point of view. The power structure was white, and these lawyers, who were also white, were seen as part of it. In a real sense, then, The Association was experienced as a political enemy to be carefully watched.

Though never baldly stated, the conception of exploiting these lawyers instead of cooperating with them was built into the language and mood that guided their encounters. It is most difficult to relate in any other way to a political opponent who at least momentarily is cast in the role of an ally. However, though they persistently stressed political factors—chiefly the conservatism of the lawyers—as the major sources of tension, the evidence during this last phase of their relationship suggested that this might not have been the major determinant. Race, followed by professional or status distinctions, seemed to loom paramount and touch more deeply.

In planning how to conduct negotiations with the Housing Authority, NAC refused to permit the white lawyers to assist them in any way; they would not even accept technical assistance. Their position was consistent with the distrust and antagonism that had developed. Certainly part of their refusal to accept assistance was a reaction to Stanley Berke's habit of occasionally asserting the advisability of his own opinions over theirs. But even Morris Rosen, who obtained for them their only legal victory, had frequently visited their community, and was regarded by them as relatively compatible politically, was excluded. In fact, at a meeting to plan for the negotiation session with the Housing Authority in Rogers Point, Morris, who had been invited by a tenant union leader from another neighborhood, was ordered to leave. Curtis told him that they could manage well enough without his assistance.

Colbert Brown, the black chief counsel of one of The Association's neighborhood offices located elsewhere in the City, initially had more success. The organizers first met him when crashing a chief counsel meeting in the main office to express their grievances. To avoid a blow-up, the lawyers attempted to steer the discussion to how both groups could work together to persuade the Housing Authority to make substantial reforms. Stanley made a proposal, which he had earlier called to their attention, for setting up a corporation of unemployed public housing residents to contract with the Housing Authority to maintain the premises. Though privately the organizers praised the plan, they finally rejected it. Stanley was still anxious to convince them of its feasibility.

> Stanley: Look, we still think this proposal may answer some of your grievances.

> Curtis: Now really, Mr. Berke, I didn't know lawyers told their clients what's best for them.

This tense meeting was becoming increasingly unmanageable until Colbert intervened. He told the organizers, firmly but politely, what steps he thought should be taken by them to settle the strike. Though he offered no ideas that they hadn't heard from Stanley, they were attentive and respectful. He had succeeded in changing the mood of the meeting. George had wanted to interrupt once, but Curtis signaled to him to remain silent. After Colbert stated his views, they warmly thanked him for his interest. They then thanked the chief counsels for their time and attention, and quietly left the meeting.

It is somewhat surprising that Colbert so readily gained the respect of the organizers, because even though he was black, he was regarded as fairly conservative. In his own community, a member organization of the city-wide Tenant Council was conducting a small rent strike. Colbert had refused to represent its tenants in court, arguing that since they would lose there was no justifiable reason for him to do so. Instead, he urged private negotiations with the Housing Authority to settle differences. The organizers knew of his refusal to fully represent the clients of one of their compatriot organizations, yet at this meeting his political record seemed to make no difference to them.

They were clearly impressed with Colbert. In anticipation of a meeting planned with the mayor, they met with him on their own initiative to formulate their strategies and demands. According to Colbert, the meeting was productive. He also reported a side of Curtis that had not been apparent to the other lawyers. He claimed that Curtis was anxiously seeking a face-saving way out of the strike. With Colbert's assistance, the organizers hammered out a reasonable program to present to the mayor.

Curtis invited Colbert to join their delegation. No other lawyer, including Morris, received an invitation. At the meeting with the mayor, which was well attended by Housing Authority officials, the antagonistic posture of one commissioner triggered an exchange of recriminations. Presenting demands right then would have been ill-advised, for tempers were high. In fact, the Rogers Point delegation almost walked out before Colbert interceded to restore order to the meeting. Playing an intermediate role, he finally suggested that the Housing Authority and NAC meet at another time in the Rogers Point Community. This arrangement, which the Housing Authority executive director welcomed as an opportunity to hear and respond to NAC's demands, was set for the following week. During most of the meeting at the mayor's office, Curtis and the other organizers remained virtually silent, permitting Colbert to negotiate on NAC's behalf. Afterward, they spoke favorably of Colbert's role, and indicated that NAC had finally been able to procure a decent lawyer.

Yet when NAC met again several days later to prepare for the negotiation session with the Housing Authority, Colbert, who assumed his presence was welcome, was asked to leave the meeting. Of course, there was nothing wrong in itself with the preference of the organizers to negotiate on their own. The mood in the City had favored the development of programs by indigenous groups working without professional assistance. But the organizers were abrupt and inconsistent, and this understandably startled Colbert. He had been actively solicited and embraced and, then, without explanation, rebuked. The tendency to shift suddenly from an all-embracing and acquiescent posture to one of firm resistance and independence has already been noted in NAC's relationship with the white attorneys. This pattern of response apparently also operated in the relationship between the organizers and Curtis; it simply took longer to unfold. Though Colbert was black, he still had professional credentials, and these posed a challenge to their self-esteem.

Finally, at the negotiation sessions in Rogers Point, the organizers threatened to abandon negotiations unless the Housing Authority was willing to accept their first demand. Colbert then quietly approached one organizer, and advised him that they should present, in their own political interest, their other grievances. The organizers reacted with anger and indignation; it seemed to them another example of professionals attempting to run the show. They generally resented being told by "outsiders" that they were making mistakes, and were especially furious when so advised by professionals. Later at their office, Curtis remarked dispararagingly that Colbert, like the other Association lawyers, was a "fink." In all future dealings with the Housing Authority, NAC dropped its contact with The Association.

CHAPTER SIX

CONCLUSION

WE HAVE just completed a painful examination of the failure of the Neighborhood Action Committee organizers to move effectively toward winning the rent strike. Forcing the Housing Authority to accede to their demands had a dual purpose for them. They believed that the conditions under which the tenants lived were abhorrent, and they considered it a major task to force the agency to change its practices and policies. NAC also wanted to build a radical black nationalist movement, and believed that a victory over these "white exploiters" would advance this long-range aim.

But NAC never developed the political muscle and influence to win. The organizers failed to build an effective organization. Tenant membership did not increase, and the striking tenants did not participate. In fact the tenants, who were relatively uninterested in the first place, became even less committed as the strike progressed. And because they did not participate and no gains were made, the strikers formed no attachment to the organization. In the city-wide community, the organizers were almost politically friendless toward the end of the strike; by then, they had fairly thoroughly discredited themselves. Finally, despite the organizers' own impressions, they never really intimidated the Housing Authority.

While losing the strike, the organizers still might have

educated the tenants politically and brought them around to their point of view. Radicals often use issues for this purpose, and NAC certainly gave lip service to that goal. To have worked in this way would have brought the organizers a step closer to their ideological aims. But NAC failed to make any progress in this regard and in fact lost a good deal of ground. The tenants were more discouraged after the strike than when they originally joined. If they learned any lessons at all, it was that "you can't fight City Hall," to say nothing about battling the system at large.

NAC's main immediate goal, winning the strike, was certainly a difficult one; even the effective mobilization of political resources carried with it no guarantees of success. Though some tenant unions have been rewarded for their efforts, many have not. Even among well-organized groups, factors such as the lack of sufficient resources, the power and ruthlessness of government agencies, and internal dissension within the community have caused incalculable political damage. Nevertheless, there is a very serious difference between organizations that "fight the good fight" and those that are too weak internally to ever stand a chance. Unfortunately, the difference often escapes the public. The media often conveys the impression that some of these groups are towers of strength, when in reality there is more noise than substance to their movement. The failure of the public, and particularly the poor, to realize this feeds the illusion that the establishment cannot be beaten. How can they, if even the strong are unable? This is tragic, but not only because it is terribly pessimistic; it is inaccurate as well.

For the sake of political clarity, then, let us admit that NAC was more noise than substance. Though it received a great deal of publicity, and many imagined it a poor man's Goliath, it suffocated internally, and despite sincerity and good intentions its armor was slight for the many battles it took on. NAC's failure to develop an effective political program was, to a great extent, a function of the behavior of the organizers. Their behavior, in turn, was shaped by two major factors: the character of their radical black nationalist ideology, and the pervasive influence of a style of relatedness based upon their social background. Both factors conspired to generate a self-defeating political pattern. In the remainder of this chapter, we shall look at how these factors operated, independently and in relation to each other, in order to explain the political conduct that has been described in the foregoing chapters.

II

NAC defined itself as a radical, black nationalist, militant organization. Its radicalism spoke to a conviction that the problems of black people could not be significantly changed without overhauling America's "racist economic and social institutions." Ghettos were more than enclaves of poor blacks; they were colonies serving white imperialism. Further, this system of exploitation could not be reformed nor compromised. The kind of new society NAC had in mind was never very clear. Though the organizers occasionally talked about socialism, this was never seriously or carefully incorporated into their ideology.

Their radicalism was linked instead to their black nationalism. They called for all-black control of the institutions that affected black people. NAC, in contrast to other black organizations which have also been demanding various forms of control, opposed seating black tenants on the Housing Authority's policy-making commission. According to NAC, it would not alter the fact of white domination, and blacks would therefore be lackeys. Their black nationalism, then, was linked to a radical perspective. But it also shared in common with other black nationalist groups a commitment to building all-black organizations. Though willing to accept white support under certain conditions, NAC was extremely distrustful of alliances with whites. With regard to militancy, the organization believed that disruptive activities, whether peaceful or not, were indispensable to achieving social change.

NAC's radicalism had a decidedly sectarian or in-group character, which greatly influenced how the organizers perceived and behaved toward others, and how others related to them. As might be expected, many organizations and individual citizens would refuse to cooperate with radicals under any conditions. But NAC appreciably exacerbated this difficulty by adopting a stance that was more often moralistic than political. Though desiring to build a movement, NAC generally did not think in terms of moving people politically. Instead, believing strongly in the moral correctness of their position, they hammered out their point of view without ever considering that the manner in which they communicated had unfavorable political consequences for them.

In presenting their ideas without being politically sensitive to their various audiences, the burden of responsibility fell upon others, for the organizers assumed that convincing others reflected not how they operated or presented themselves, but whether those whom they addressed were decent political types. Another important aspect of their moral radicalism was the tendency to believe that those more moderate than themselves were either "sell-outs" or dupes, and were therefore potential enemies or at best untrustworthy allies. These perspectives, which were taken very seriously, generated indifference and antagonism between themselves and others.

Several key groups who were quite sympathetic to the aims of reforming the Housing Authority refused to associate themselves with NAC. An outstanding example was the refusal of the militant issue-oriented South Peak Tenants Union to respond favorably to NAC's overtures. There was some ambivalence and hedging at first, but NAC was finally rejected because it was considered by the tenant union as "too far out in left field." Its leaders were disturbed both by the radical politics of NAC and by the brazen style in which the organizers communicated their views. The South Peak Tenants Union, which eventually won its own strike, had feared that associating with NAC would injure its own reputation. So, interestingly enough, even a militant group willing to use direct action tactics still considered a connection with NAC politically damaging.

There were, nevertheless, some moderate black groups who were interested in cooperating with NAC, but they were treated with what appeared to be crass expediency because they were defined as liberal organizations. NAC's relationship with a moderate black rent-strike leader, whose concern with his own rent strike did not extend beyond winning reforms, was noted earlier. Not only were his goals too limited for NAC, but the organizers resented his willingness to meet privately, all alone, with the Housing Authority. On the other hand, he was quite willing to engage in a joint venture with NAC. Their outspoken radical politics and abrasive style did not trouble him. He apparently believed, perhaps naively, that a great deal was to be gained, or certainly nothing lost, by assuming that almost everyone was a potential ally.

The Rogers Point organizers were greatly troubled by his liberal politics. His views were treated with disdain, anger, and mockery. Privately, they referred to him as a "fink." What made their attitude toward him significant was that they never took his views and formal proposals seriously, and when it was to their advantage they ignored him. Without his knowledge, they excluded him from meetings that had a direct bearing on his own situation. They rarely attempted to try to convince him in a patient way that he was erring politically.

The reason they carried on any sort of relationship with the "fink" was because they found him occasionally useful. When they needed pickets or a delegation to meet with public officials, they were able to count on their liberal ally, who was also affiliated with the city-wide Tenant Council, to bring people along. However, despite his patience, he eventually became disillusioned. It became apparent to him that the gains achieved by allying with NAC were one-sided, and probably more important, he resented NAC's discourteousness. He broke off his ties with NAC, which did not regret the move.

The nationalist character of NAC further narrowed its range of potential allies. The organizers were opposed to building political ties with white citizens and organizations in a city where blacks were in a minority. Their nationalist ideology, which interpreted basic cleavages in racial terms, not only tended to make them shun alliances with influential middle-class groups but even caused them to avoid ties with some poor people's organizations.

Generally speaking, black nationalist organizations have occasionally drawn upon the support of white radicals, who have been about the only group ready to offer blacks unqualified support. But aside from the students in Presentation City, with whom the organizers preferred not to associate politically, there was really no radical community they could have readily drawn upon. It was not their policy to automatically reject white support, but the terms they would impose for accepting any assistance were so stringent that very few white citizens or groups would be willing to accept them. They were willing, for example, to ally with white lawyers, but only on their own terms.

A more complicated consequence of this nationalist ethos was the impact it had upon the internal character of NAC. The commitment to black nationalism was a major factor in maintaining cohesion and even preventing the organization from falling apart. At the same time, it made NAC more politically rigid. We have already seen how Curtis Jones gained the political loyalty of the other organizers in his battles against the poverty program administrators by interpreting major political differences that existed between NAC and those with whom they disagreed as based on racial antagonism. As the oldest and most experienced of the organizers, Curtis was able to shrewdly link nationalist issues to his radical politics. This was no cynical maneuver; it reflected his political views. Nevertheless, if any of the organizers had challenged Curtis, who was putting himself out on a limb in his battles with non-black members of the community, it would have been interpreted by all as a betrayal. Curtis succeeded in creating a political atmosphere within his organization that made it virtually impossible to openly challenge any of his political positions.

However, there were differences in political opinion between the individual organizers, and a great deal of personal tension between them as well. These factors exerted a centrifugal pull on the organization. On the whole, maintaining the unity of the organization by stressing black nationalism was successful. But the nationalist ethos tended, though not always successfully, to relegate personal tensions and political differences to a covert level, which in turn prompted an overt behavioral pattern that may be characterized as rigid.

What seems to have occurred was this: the gap between the black unity norms of the nationalist ethos and the organizers' actual estrangement from each other prompted them to over-conform. Sensing their own differences and interpersonal tensions, they cautiously avoided letting on to others and themselves the fragile character of their social bond. Frequent and intense discussions among the organizers on the importance of black people getting along and working together left no doubt about the great meaning they attached to the nationalist value. In political terms, this meant having good working relations with each other and being united behind a single political perspective. For blacks to be incompatible, either personally or politically, was anathema to their commitment to black unity.

In their personal relations with each other, there were two major signs of trouble. First, they were extremely competitive. Though acting as a team in public, privately each of the organizers would enjoy boasting about his own individual contributions as compared to those of the others. George Franklyn, for example, continually exclaimed that he, more than the other organizers, was really responsible for the strike. He reasoned that the good reputation he had earned as a tenant in the project explained why some tenants were willing to join the strike. Believing that he excelled the others, though, was not only a boast. George also felt it as a burden. He thought that he carried too large a share of the load and that his efforts were unappreciated by the others. So when discussing his contributions as an organizer, the tone of his remarks reflected anger as well as vanity.

Second, the mutual distrust between the organizers seemed deep; I had the distinct sense that they really didn't like each other. Elliot Liebow made a similar observation in his study of a black street-corner group. He noted that despite frequent claims of close personal ties, "friendship does not often stand up well to the stress of crisis or conflict of interest when demands tend to be heaviest and most insistent."* He also observed that friendship, though often addressed as if it is a sacred covenant, is at another level recognized as the locus of cynical exploitation.† As with Liebow's street-corner men, there was often a substantial gap between the claims and the behavior of the organizers.

In private, they often spoke about each other in highly critical terms, and even believed themselves to be victims of the others' deviousness. For example, Jerry Cook once suspected that Eddie Daniels was plotting to get him fired. He imagined, among other things, that Eddie was jealous because he and George were then getting on well with each other. On another occasion, Jerry and Eddie were outraged by George's temper tantrums. Something was always going haywire between them, and these tensions posed a serious threat to NAC's unity.

Curtis finally instituted "bitching sessions" to provide the organizers with an opportunity to unload their tensions. These meetings would continue until their differences were at least formally resolved. Curtis would always stress at these meetings, as well as on other occasions, how important it was for blacks to get along with each other. For whatever their apparent differences, those with their enemies were much greater. But the interpersonal tensions that surfaced at these meetings hardly exhausted the harsh feelings that they harbored toward each other. Occasionally shaking hands afterward to show that all was forgiven often seemed more a formality than a relaxed exchange. And no matter how much tension was released on these occasions, it would invariably develop again soon.

It is not surprising that they strained to show a unified

---

* Elliot Liebow, *Tally's Corner* (Boston, 1967), p. 180.
† Liebow, p. 181.

political perspective, particularly when we consider that political differences, like their interpersonal tensions, existed between them despite their unwavering commitment to black unity. For the organizers, political differences posed a more sensitive issue than personality matters, and how this was handled reflected that sensitivity. Interestingly enough, though the organizers expressed opinions that were departures from the prevailing views, they were, somehow, able to shut out the realization that their opinions did in fact clash.

For example, George once mentioned to me the importance of stressing a cultural as opposed to a political orientation in improving the conditions of black people. When I told him that this view stood in opposition to NAC's official political position, he seemed startled and became visibly embarrassed. More dramatic was Eddie Daniels' reaction when I confronted him with the differences between his own expressed views and those of the other organizers on a particular issue. He actually panicked, became visibly shaken, and blurted out how dedicated he was to the organization. He apparently interpreted having any difference of opinion as a sign of disloyalty.

In public, they always seemed to be of one mind, with each always reinforcing the others. A perceptive observer would notice that even when one of the organizers would make a remark that was too inaudible or rambling to be heard, at least one of the other organizers would still shout approval. These confrontations often appeared to others as vigorous and overacted performances. It seems that a sensing of their differences generated internal psychological pressure for each to play the proper role demanded by the nationalist ethos, with its stress on black unity.

The role-playing that characterized their behavior when confronting outsiders also guided their behavior toward each other. There was an unstated agreement not to be critical of each other's behavior, and whenever possible to be highly supportive. So George Franklyn would praise Eddie Daniels for a leaflet he had written, though he privately expressed concern that the statement had overlooked a major issue. And when one organizer proposed a plan of action, unless tempers were high the others tended to avoid directly challenging its advisability. This situation severely limited their political flexibility by narrowing down the range of political alternatives that they could feel comfortable about considering.

On one major policy, however, they all genuinely agreed—that beating the establishment required moving beyond the framework of conventional politics. Black people had to engage in militant or direct action tactics. They were convinced that the chances of significantly improving conditions in public housing were directly related to the extent to which they could continually disrupt the normal operation of the Housing Authority and the City. So although it was not reflected in practice, they firmly believed that their main task was to build a large organization of tenants who were ready, willing, and able to cooperate and take risks.

The barriers to building an organization in this ghetto community were formidable. The neighborhood was fairly atomized, with little formal or informal group life. Tenant apathy was pervasive, and few were normally willing to take any action that might bring eviction. Under these circumstances, the day-to-day task of organizing tenants was bound to be extremely difficult and tedious. To stand even a chance of putting together the kind of organization that NAC had in mind would necessarily require a considerable amount of organizing skill, self-discipline, and personal endurance.

NAC's reputation as a revolutionary organization further minimized its chances of increasing tenant participation. Tenant dissatisfaction with conditions did not, of course, necessarily imply a readiness to favor radical solutions to social problems. Tenants were interested in immediate improvements in housing conditions. Though the energies of the organization were oriented mainly around this goal, it was difficult for tenants to ignore NAC's radical character. The kind of leaflets the organizers distributed and the political commitments they expressed to tenants undoubtedly frightened many away. On the other hand, NAC offered only slogans and made no systematic efforts to radicalize the tenants.

NAC's ideology, then, under the conditions in which it operated, worked against its own interests in winning the strike. With very little potential for building their own political base or winning allies in the City, and lacking the kind of organization that could encourage open discussion among its organizers, which then might have increased its tactical flexibility, NAC was rendered virtually powerless and without influence. Lacking political power, influence, and even a good reputation, NAC was placed in a political box in which almost anything it did would tend to be politically self-defeating; no activities the organizers engaged in would bring them closer to winning the strike. It is not surprising, then, that their powerlessness, to which they contributed considerably, would produce enormous feelings of frustration and anger, which in turn were reflected in their political behavior.

In other words, their powerlessness generated behavior that was often motivated by a sense of frustration rather than by norms of political expediency. They would engage in activities that served to gratify various immediate needs, such as release of tension. Ironically, just as the ideological straight-jacket encouraged expressive behavior, their ideology also fostered non-utilitarian behavior by liberating them from restrictions. By not developing allies in the City or a substantial base in their own community, they were not subject to the expectations of others, who might have demanded that they pursue a different political course of action as a price for their support.

At the end of the strike, George Franklyn said that it could have continued if many of the tenants had not stopped turning over their rent payments to NAC. The tenants were rebelling against NAC, which caused the organizers to close shop perhaps earlier than they had wanted. No matter what the organizers thought of the tenants, they were in some ways subject to their pressure. Had the tenants been organized and meeting together all along, they would have been in a position to ask questions, make suggestions, and even challenge the conduct of the strike itself. NAC might have been forced to behave differently.

Indeed, having no significant ties encouraged them to become not active organizers but angry spokesmen. Their activities became largely confined to exercises in radical and militant rhetoric. Rather than engaging in the unquestionably arduous task of organizing tenants, they took on the highly visible spokesman role of making speeches—usually dramatic ones—issuing press releases, holding press conferences, and engaging in heated verbal exchanges with establishment officials. In truth, they were organizers in name only.

III

Though the nature of an organization's ideological commitment may provide a sufficient basis for the structuring of both expressive and self-defeating political behavior, it did not, in fact, adequately account for many of NAC's activities, including those that often appeared to be politically motivated. Since the barriers to building an organization were undoubtedly formidable, the organizers might have tried harder in several ways. They might have spent more time and energy in actual organizing efforts. They might have thought through their strategies carefully and reevaluated them during the course of the strike. And, within the framework of their ideology, they might have behaved toward the Housing Authority, lawyers, and others in a manner more consistent with their political interests. But as we have seen, their efforts in these various directions were minimal.

Rather, it often appeared that the ideology itself was conveniently shaped and defined to serve social and psychological needs. The enormous weight of these politically nonutilitarian influences, though almost never apparent to the organizers, crucially inhibited the development of a potentially effective political program. In this section, I will draw upon the empirical material to identify these factors and sketch in how they operated.

Before proceeding, it will be useful to keep in mind a broader issue, which will be taken up more fully in the next section. The major characteristics of the organizers have been also observed by many researchers in other lower class male groups, that is those which are relatively marginal to the labor force. While there is general agreement that significant sections of the poor display certain common patterns of behavior, social scientists differ as to the derivation of these characteristics. The major debate is whether these behavioral uniformities constitute a lower class culture or whether they are adaptations to social and economic conditions and readily amenable to being modified or transformed if conditions are changed. We shall return to this issue later.

When we consider the major ideological commitment of NAC to raising the level of political consciousness and confidence of the striking tenants, the manner in which Jerry Cook and the other organizers actually related to the tenants offered impressive testimony to the immense sway of non-political factors. We have already seen how Jerry Cook's series of sexual encounters with various striking tenants operated to discourage regular meetings of the tenants. Why did he not restrict these encounters, in the interest of the political goals of the organization, to women who resided elsewhere, or at the very least to those who had clearly no intentions of joining the strike? The reason was simply that the striking women were more accessible to him. Unless he had been subject to counter-pressures from the other organizers, which was never the case, it would not have occurred to him to behave otherwise.

Interestingly, even though Jerry Cook admitted that his opposition to having tenants meet in a group at NAC's office reflected his personal interests, he still attempted to interpret his behavior as conforming to the political program of NAC. He claimed that visiting tenants in their own homes amounted to holding political meetings, since strike-related issues were discussed. Jerry was certainly not as politically minded as, say, Curtis Jones. But he did consider himself a loyal member of NAC and genuinely believed that the abuses of the Housing Authority against the tenants should be drastically curbed. So he was not simply making facile excuses by justifying his behavior on ideological grounds. He really believed his line of argument, which in effect tailored the ideology to fit his personal style.

In working to keep the tenants on strike, he persistently withheld information, distorted and fabricated facts, and instilled fear. To a certain extent, this strategy was forced upon him. The decision to keep the tenants politically isolated naturally bred considerable anxiety among them about their situation. They needed reassurance, which could not have been readily offered by accurately reporting the facts of the strike. The claim, for example, that the Housing Authority was on the verge of conceding was patently false and would not stand up. Jerry was indeed in a most difficult situation. But it would have been very difficult for him to have behaved in a straightforward fashion. Putting others on was how he normally operated. He gained a great deal of satisfaction from what seemed to him his clever behavior, and he often boasted about his various on-the-spot ruses.

If Jerry Cook was deviating from some of NAC's political objectives, why didn't the other organizers object? They repeatedly stated, both publicly and privately, that NAC's major indictment of white society was its failure to permit black people to determine their own destiny. The organizers also criticized black leaders who did not consult with community people on issues affecting them. And, as Curtis himself would often put it when objecting to a particular political position, "the tenants would never stand for it."

But we know that he made no serious attempts to gauge tenant opinion on issues, nor did he or the others attempt to develop structures that would make the views of the strikers known to them. Clearly, the ideology of the organizers, on the one hand, and how they actually behaved, on the other, were at odds with each other. It is in this context that we can understand why the others accepted the manner in which Jerry Cook related to the tenants.

First, the organizers took seriously the division of labor they had set up among themselves, which generally implied a mutual non-interference policy. Though each organizer was occasionally criticized by the others, these criticisms were neither frequent nor basic. None of them took well to rebuffs, and too much internal criticism would have posed serious threats to the unity of the organization, which they seemed to sense. Second, it was implicit in the way they viewed Jerry's work that they did not basically respect their female constituency. Certainly, to have permitted the strikers to participate fully would have been especially threatening to these men, for all of them had lower class backgrounds, with the often attendant doubts about their abilities to assume masculine roles. But the tenants were denied not only full participation but even the most elementary courtesies. In truth, they were subject to a great deal of exploitation.

Jerry flitted from one affair to another because they were inherently unstable relationships. But an important aspect of Jerry's style was the importance of sexual domination to his masculine image. There was nothing subtle about this. He clearly thought of himself as a lady's man, and enjoyed playing that role. Domination and conquest were also important to the other organizers, but they expressed this differently.

A rare meeting in which several tenants were invited to attend a joint get-together with another group elsewhere in the City was quite revealing. Throughout the meeting, the women who attempted to speak were either ignored or interrupted. Although tenants had been invited, the organizers behaved as if they really had no right to be present. The reason some tenants were invited in the first place was that the organizers felt an obligation to the other rent strike leader, with whom they had agreed to hold a joint meeting in his community. NAC believed that it fulfilled its end of the bargain by bringing along, in effect, several bodies.

During the entire meeting, the organizers were forceful and dominating. The women were urged not to become too anxious and to remain on strike. The organizers insisted that they knew best. In truth, I had expected that the organizers would at least go through the motions of permitting participation, but they did not. They were unquestionably asserting their masculinity, as they defined it, which meant nothing less than dominating the affairs of the women. In this broader sense, they related to women somewhat as Jerry Cook did. Perhaps this is why, on several occasions when tenants bypassed Jerry and contacted the office directly to complain, the organizers were generally offended and informed the women in strong language who was making decisions. In short, to the extent that their social style weighed more heavily than ideological considerations, one could expect the organizers to remain, essentially, uncritical of Jerry's behavior.

But how did the organizers themselves reconcile the stark discrepancy between their ideological dictates and their actual behavior? Simply, they did not acknowledge that a significant gap existed. Generally speaking, politically active persons of any persuasion are convinced of their own integrity and consistency. These organizers were not cynics. They tended to define and evaluate their relations with the external world in terms of the feelings that animated them. What they felt was real to them. Feeling that they were radical, fair, and courageous provided its own affirmation.

Though the organizers believed that they were better able to deal with the world of politics than the tenants, they would never admit that they viewed the women tenants as objects of manipulation. As for Jerry Cook's role, the organizers claimed that he was keeping the tenants informed and that they were encouraged to express their concerns through him or, if necessary, by contacting the office directly. In this regard, I asked George Franklyn why NAC did not hold joint tenant meetings. He claimed that this would be very inconvenient for the tenants, who were virtually all mothers living alone with their children; he said they could not really obtain babysitters. In short, the organizers did not see the gap between word and deed as serious. To the extent that they could acknowledge a gap at all, they saw it as naturally rooted in the limits of the situation rather than as a moral violation of a political commitment.

The gap between the intentions of the organizers and their actual accomplishments was most seriously reflected in their failure to develop a numerically substantial base, and one that could be mobilized to participate in militant action. Without an effective organization, the possibility of forcing the Housing Authority to accede to their demands was small. The organizers were convinced that they were doing a good organizing job, but their perceptions did not change the reality that failing to build a base would cost them the advantages inherent in political power.

Had they adhered more strictly to their militant point of view, they might have worked along with Jerry Cook to recruit more tenants. The reason that they spurned such efforts despite the potential advantages was no mystery. The organizers preferred to talk about organizing rather than actually engaging in it. Organizing demands a considerable degree of self-discipline, and the willingness to invest considerable time in tasks that are often tedious and only occasionally dramatic. Virtually none of these attributes characterized the organizers.

Further, their own lower class background, as reflected in the problems raised by having had to engage in menial and low status occupations, apparently touched a sensitive chord. They resisted performing tasks that might serve as reminders of such work. Ironically, though they called themselves organizers, they did not consider the kind of work that went into the day-to-day tasks of organizing as dignified. They had very definite ideas on the ranking of roles within a political organization. Their main division was between mental and physical work. Mental work was highly valued while physical work was frowned upon. Physical tasks were not to be allocated to the most gifted and talented members, which included, according to them, all but Jerry Cook.

Whatever pride Jerry Cook may have derived from his dealings with the tenants as an organizer, he was largely defined by the other organizers as a runner, whose main task was to cover the physical territory of the project. This message was communicated by the sort of remarks they made to him, and, significantly, by those that weren't. "Jerry, did you cover the other side of the hill yet? Mrs. Adams called and said you didn't pick up her rent yet." Or, perhaps more poignant, Curtis Jones once remarked, "I'm not saying you ain't doing a good job, but if you didn't spend so much time bullshitting with each tenant, you'd get more done." Never were any comments made to Jerry expressing concern whether particular tenants better understood the point of view of the organization, to say nothing about inquiring generally about their political development. They never expressed any confidence that Jerry could perform such a mission. The remarks about his work generally implied that he was engaging in labor that involved, essentially, little thought or intelligence.

The other organizers were the "brains." While there was an overlapping of responsibilities, each had designated tasks. Eddie Daniels wrote the leaflets, George Franklyn did most of the speaking, and Curtis Jones was mainly responsible for planning strategies, though he, too, often spoke in public. They all considered their work demanding, but only in the sense that it involved ingenuity and verbal abilities. Jerry Cook's job also required mental agility, for keeping the tenants on strike was a very difficult task, but none of the other organizers looked at it quite that way.

The net effect of their operation was to make the organizers spokesmen, leaders whose main task was not organizing but engaging in symbolic conflict encounters. I have already discussed how the impact of their ideology under the conditions in which they operated independently favored the spokesman role. What also occurred was that, in deference to the various non-political pulls on their behavior, their ideology was redefined to legitimize the spokesman role as the major outlet for their political energy. Being militant, then, meant primarily telling the establishment off in very strong language, while their radical nationalism was essentially something to be publicly flaunted. The organizers, in truth, were less interested in building a movement than in creating an image. A certain degree of magical thinking reinforced the legitimacy of their political role as spokesmen. Imagination, in other words, substituted for activity. As George Franklyn said, "If they get tough with us, we can always get the troops out." His claim, of course, was baseless, but it did serve to rationalize not engaging in the task of organizing.

Rather than conducting an active recruiting drive, we have seen how the organizers, instead, exaggerated the number of strikers. They thought this ruse would be successful for two reasons. First, the Housing Authority director impressed them, by reputation and later by his dealings with them, as a person of fairly low intelligence who could be readily fooled; his easy-going manner suggested to them that he was "not on the ball" and could be easily intimidated. What they failed to realize was that their estimate of him was not relevant. It did not seriously occur to them that there was an elaborate bureaucratic machine that operated independently of the executive director, and which computed fairly accurately the real extent of rent delinquency.

Second, the tremendous gratification they gained by believing that they had outsmarted the Housing Authority persuaded them that they were behaving practically. They continued to make exaggerated claims of the number of strikers even after they realized that their earlier claims had been discovered to be false. As with Jerry Cook, putting on others was a style of relating that could not readily be dropped despite the disadvantages entailed.

The specific character of their spokesman role was shaped largely by three distinctive orientations, which despite appearances were not derived from their political ideology. First, great emphasis was placed on exhibiting a tough exterior, one which displayed such qualities as fearlessness and bravery. Second, it appeared urgent to the organizers to demonstrate their autonomy, and accordingly to show their resistance to authority. Third, there was a pressing tendency to seek out situations that promised much stimulation and excitement. Each of these orientations will be considered in turn.

The many confrontations the organizers had with the Housing Authority reveal the importance they attached to appearing tough. During many of the meetings of the agency's commission, they threatened its members, defied warnings, and continually disrupted the proceedings. Of course, this kind of behavior is often implied in a politically militant stance. However, the post-meeting conversations of the organizers, which I have likened to little victory celebrations, suggest that politically motivated factors were not the essential sources of their behavior. Only rarely during their discussions afterward did they address themselves to the political concerns that others assumed accounted for their conduct at the Housing Authority meetings. Certainly, they were concerned with scoring political points. But the conversational stress and mutual back-patting that characterized these sessions had little to do with political issues.

Here are some typical comments that they exchanged: "Man, we made them shit in their pants"; "Who are they kidding? They'd need an army to kick us out of those meetings." In referring to a commissioner: "I felt like belting Ackerman's pusser. And you know, I bet he'd just keep on smiling." With regard to the executive director: "Man, did you see O'Rourke's face and listen to that sissy talk. He's not *that* dumb to take us on." The organizers were clearly showing how tough they were, even when confronting men of power.

It was interesting to hear that the organizers were convinced they had successfully intimidated the commissioners. As was often the case when they gauged the reaction of their opponents, they were wrong. In these instances, they observed that the agency members did not exhibit much anger. Instead, the organizers were treated politely and respectfully, though it was obvious that their behavior was regarded as improper. The moderation and self-restraint of the agency officials, essentially, reflected adherence to bureaucratic norms and was not, as the organizers suspected, a fear response. The organizers mistakenly evaluated the reaction of the commissioners according to the criteria they would have applied to themselves had they behaved similarly.

Returning to the little victory celebrations, I had originally assumed that they represented a much greater sensitivity to the political issues than they really did. For example, "we made them shit in their pants" could have been not only a boast but an observation that their efforts to convince the Housing Authority of their political strength were successful. But if their motives were primarily political, they would have discussed means of capitalizing on the agency's fears. They never did. In this case, as in many others, they did not propose any follow-up on their presumed success. Significantly, their successive confrontations with the Housing Authority seemed generally repetitious. They made no attempts to continue the dialogue with the agency in ways that would incorporate the events of previous meetings. This lack of continuity reflected their lack of interest in evaluating the activities that occupied their political energies.

From the point of view of those who saw them in action, their tough stance conveyed the image of a stern, "no holds barred" group. Again, though this is characteristic of militants, the main sources of the organizers' behavior were not political. Many, however, thought they were. Observers also interpreted as politically motivated certain actions which were, in fact, largely shaped by the organizers' pursuit of excitement. Seeking excitement gave their behavior an unusual degree of intensity, which made them often seem much more serious politically than they really were; also, they would appear at various places quite unexpectedly, leaving others to guess what political motives were involved.

To cite one instance, I saw one morning at their office how a desire for an exciting venture swiftly moved them from a state of boredom to animation. For no apparent reason, George Franklyn blurted out to the others, who all seemed bored, "Hey, let's go downtown and give that fuck Douglas Edwards hell. You know, he promised to do something about those lists of complaints we gave him. And we're still waiting around." One might have thought he had uttered magic words. His suggestion brought them quickly to life, and we all rushed down to the Housing Authority.

They dashed into the office of the assistant director, Douglas, but he wasn't there. They then attempted, quite noisily, to barge into O'Rourke's office, but his secretary insisted that he was at a meeting elsewhere. They marched back and forth through the hallways of the Housing Authority attempting to find one of the major administrators. It was a frantic scene. The organizers eventually returned to Edwards' office, and one of them waved his finger at the secretary, warning that they would be returning soon.

Upon speaking later to Mr. Edwards' secretary, I learned that she thought they wanted to be thrown out to cause the Housing Authority trouble and inflame the black community. But she was attributing more political rationality to this incident than actually existed. A "joy ride" would be a far more appropriate analogue to what occurred. Once outside the Housing Authority, the organizers appeared quite exhilarated. This experience was apparently cathartic and everyone departed in high spirits.

Their almost continuous search for stimulation, which generated behavior that was highly impulsive and frantic, often seemed to others to reflect their ultra-militancy. But to convince the opposition of one's militancy is not tantamount to intimidating them. Another conclusion could be drawn, particularly when a militant stance is not actually supported by any evidence of power — namely, that the militants can be safely ignored, or if necessary easily crushed.

A third major orientation was the stress they placed on autonomy. Though their desire to exhibit independence often prevailed over political concerns, this posture tended to be politically interpreted. It gave the impression to others that NAC was composed of ideologues whose politics permitted no compromise. Under the influence of Curtis Jones, NAC's politics certainly hardened ideologically, but the great extent to which their hard, unbending line reflected non-political factors was hidden from others.

The public negotiation session held in the Rogers Point community between NAC and the Housing Authority has already been described. Though the agency's executive director, O'Rourke, had implicitly acceded to their first demand that no evictions take place during negotiations, they still insisted upon a formal declaration. When O'Rourke suggested moving to the next item on the agenda, the organizers abruptly brought the meeting to an end. Afterwards, I returned with them to their office, where they spoke of their victory over the Housing Authority. Curtis exclaimed, "We showed them who's boss," and George Franklyn added, "We're sick of them telling us what to do. It's about time we give the orders."

In fact, the organizers had prepared the agenda, without consulting the Housing Authority, and O'Rourke, after granting, in effect, their first demand, suggested that they proceed to state their other concerns. Even the tone taken by the Housing Authority representatives was conciliatory. Undoubtedly, they wanted a good press; newsmen were present. Whatever their motives, they were cooperative. Nevertheless, the organizers interpreted the events that occurred as evidence that the Housing Authority was infringing upon their autonomy and independence.

The stress on autonomy played havoc between the organizers and the lawyers. Though the organizers never openly admitted it, there were many indications that they felt considerable relief in sharing some of their burdens with The Association. But, their stress on autonomy made it very distasteful to them to acknowledge this. The organizers were extremely sensitive to any implications of dependence. They often emphasized how well they could get along on their own. Yet in seeking out lawyers, who had special skills, they put themselves in a situation of actual dependence. Add to this the important fact that they defined these lawyers as potential enemies, and later on as actual ones, and it is clear why any suggestion of dependence was bound to be repugnant to them.

We noted how the organizers would swiftly oscillate from a relatively obsequious posture toward the lawyers to one of antagonism or withdrawal. We also observed how these vacillations followed a distinct pattern. Soon after adopting a posture of dependence and acquiescence, which the lawyers thought made them "good clients," they would react with antagonism, though no apparent intervening event could explain this about-face. The evidence certainly suggests that when these dependency needs surfaced, they created personal crises for organizers and prompted political blow-ups. Their reaction was greatly inflamed by the abrasive fact that black nationalists were depending upon white professionals for help.

Finally, and extremely important, underlying the various characteristics described in this section, such as concern with autonomy and stress on toughness, was the highly expressive character of the organizers' behavior. Rather than orienting them toward political ends, these characteristic modes of behavior became ends in themselves, with each providing its own structure for gratifying specific needs.

Exploring the many non-political factors for understanding how the organizers operated, though, was not generally how others explained their political behavior. The lawyers, like the Housing Authority officials, eventually concluded that the organizers were political ideologues with no interest in reaching a political settlement. The organizers themselves had a very similar interpretation of their own behavior, though with a much more sympathetic slant—that they were committed to a political ideology that embodied a systematic philosophy geared toward making basic and large-scale changes in the society. This meant that they could not be bought off or compromised. It was therefore no surprise to them that they made many enemies and isolated allies who, in their opinion, eventually exposed themselves as false friends. The organizers never suspected throughout the fourteen-month strike that their political behavior could have been motivated by anything other than political considerations.

IV

The major behavioral patterns observed among the NAC organizers are also characteristic of a significant number of lower class males in other ethnic groups. Researchers differ on how to interpret this behavior, but the empirical findings unambiguously reveal class-related social patterns. One major conclusion that can be drawn from the extensive research on this subject is that behavior believed to be distinctively characteristic of blacks appears widely among lower class groups, regardless of race. Though the various national groups certainly have their own unique cultural and social configurations, exposure to broadly similar social and economic conditions apparently generates specific uniform adaptations.

Undoubtedly, the pervasive experience of racial discrimination has had a very special impact upon black people. It most certainly has had an important bearing upon the institutional and personal resources available to them, both in extent and in kind. And together with their poverty, it has given black people a very high potential for social protest. In this study, we have seen how the race issue shaped the character of their struggle, which is particularly well reflected in their black nationalist ethos. But certainly the most damaging consequence of racial discrimination has been the denial of stable, adequately paying job opportunities, for this has been mainly responsible for the extensive poverty and deprivation among black people. This lower class status imposed upon many blacks has had its own independent social and psychological consequences on behavior, which has important parallels among other lower class groups.

The poverty program provided the Rogers Point organizers with their first dignified and relatively well-paid jobs. All of the organizers had experienced continual financial distress, shifting back and forth from unemployment to low-paying and low-status jobs. There were important background differences among them, however. Jerry Cook fitted most closely the stereotype we have of lower class males. The others were relatively upward mobile, particularly Curtis Jones and George Franklyn, who had attended, though never completed, college. Still, despite their differences with Jerry Cook, the other three organizers never escaped the influence of their lower-class background.

Racial segregation in housing makes it much more difficult for blacks than for other groups to break away from lower-class patterns. Unlike white communities, where housing tends to be segregated according to income, the ghettos entrap all but the wealthiest blacks. This encourages contact between the economic classes, if not always among adults then at least among their children, both in school and on the streets. In Presentation City, ghetto parents frequently complain about their children's association with "bad boys." Insofar as the social climate of the ghetto is defined by its larger lower-class population, the small black middle class is much more likely to be influenced by its less economically fortunate peers, rather than the other way around. And because of their enforced isolation and confinement, the behavior patterns of the lower-class members of the community are generally subject to considerable reinforcement.

The more mobile NAC organizers, who were all raised and still reside in black ghettos, might not have behaved very differently even if their social origins had been middle-class. At least, their chance of doing so would have been substantially less than among middle-class whites. But their origins were lower-class and apparently the influence of the ghetto environment has inhibited them from abandoning a style of behavior associated with lower-class groups.

However, to say that a significant number of lower-class individuals reveal a certain set of characteristics is *not* tantamount to claiming that this applies to virtually all or most of them. Rather, various observable styles are more likely to appear among those in the lower class than in the middle or other classes. To recognize that we are not discussing an entire class has important implications. For one thing, we may avoid the impression of manufacturing social science stereotypes such as those in several reports claiming to describe the general deteriorated state of the black family, when statistically speaking, their findings apply to only a minority of black families.

Second, and especially important for our purposes, there is explanatory significance in appreciating the wide range of adaptations within the lower-class to social and economic circumstances. We then realize that class membership does not automatically mandate any characteristics or modes of behavior. And we can avoid the serious error, indeed the tautology, of labeling those poor in whom certain characteristics are absent as necessarily middle-class. It is a serious intellectual oversight, as well as a blatant form of ethnocentrism, to call certain presumably undesirable characteristics lower-class and view allegedly welcome departures from these patterns, such as the desire to have a stable family life, as automatic evidence of middle-class influence.

Of course, it might be so. However, we must take

care to avoid the implication that the desire and effort to improve one's economic status means that he has become predominantly middle-class and has therefore simply left behind his lower-class past. All the organizers, including Jerry Cook, very much wanted stable, self-respecting jobs, but their behavior cannot be described as typifying what are often identified as middle-class patterns. Furthermore, to consider some of these organizers, or other lower-class individuals as well, as middle class because some aspect of their behavior seems to resemble middle-class behavior, incurs the serious risk of interpreting many of their other patterns from a perspective that actually does not apply to them.

Keeping these things in mind, we will look at two major explanations for the patterns of behavior described in the previous section and detailed throughout the book, patterns which have been identified as lower-class. One school of thought argues that a lower-class culture exists, with various patterns which conspire to perpetuate the social and economic circumstances of the poor. According to this view, merely improving objective conditions for the lower class would not in itself crack the culture of poverty, because the life style of the poor is too deeply imbedded to enable them to readily take advantage of improved opportunities.

An alternative view, generally referred to as the structural position, directly challenges the culture of poverty argument by asserting that the key factor inhibiting the poor is lack of opportunity. The behavior of the poor, accordingly, represents an adaptation to conditions which, if changed, would also change their behavior. According to the structural position, the poor are already prepared to take advantage of improved circumstances, but are unable to only because circumstances have not readily improved. Elliot Liebow, a leading proponent of this line of argument, concludes in his study of black streetcorner men that the black poor do not constitute a distinctive subculture but are responding to their failure in terms of the values of the larger American culture. He writes: "many similarities between the lower-class Negro father and son or mother and daughter do not result from 'cultural transmission' but from the fact that the son goes out and independently experiences the same failures, in the same areas, and for very much the same reasons as his father."

While these positions are not always presented as mutually exclusive, one tends to be favored over the other. For example, although Daniel P. Moynihan agrees that conditions beyond the control of black people have been originally responsible for their extensive poverty, he claims that even in the absence of these conditions their poverty is being perpetuated because they have internalized self-defeating patterns. There are, indeed, numerous variations to both major positions. But, in general, investigators of the issue of poverty tend to be divided between those who view the group's way of life as the main bottleneck to social change, and those who identify the key trouble spot in the system itself.

These contending perspectives have tended to become ideologically loaded. That is, each particular stance is interpreted by both social scientists and the public to be an indication of one's political biases, revealing whether the investigator is sympathetic or antagonistic toward the establishment. The infusion of politics into this issue has tended to inhibit closer scrutiny of both sides of the debate. There are limits and advantages to each position that deserve attention.

When considering the structural interpretation of pov-

---

* Liebow, *Tally's Corner* (Boston, 1967), p. 222.

erty and deprivation, the evidence clearly supports its main contention—that the poor, on the whole, are willing and capable of work. Claims that high unemployment is causally related to various characteristics of individuals and groups seem highly questionable. In 1968, when most of the data for this study were gathered, unemployment for the entire labor force was officially under 2 per cent for those males in their prime working years (twenty-five to fifty-four).* For blacks only, in the comparable age group, the figure was well under 4 per cent. The Department of Labor tends to understate the extent of unemployment, but using the official rates to compare one period with another, we learn how responsive the unemployment rate is to labor market conditions. Rates for other years, for both blacks and whites, have been more than double those just cited, and since 1968 they have been rising again. Unless we are to assume that the culture of poverty changes from one year to another, and that the low 1968 rate largely reflected a temporary breakdown in its functional patterns, then we must agree that variations in the unemployment rates reflect changes in available job opportunities.

But unemployment is not the only important measure of a group's relations to the labor force. It has been argued that the lower-class cultures intervenes in two other ways. First, the inadequate wages of the poor, particularly blacks, is said to reflect their inability to take advantage of training and educational opportunities. Second, it is claimed that many poor are unemployed not because they have been seeking jobs in vain but because they have no desire to work, and wouldn't do so even if opportunities were available for them. Among other lower-class attributes presumably related to the culture of the poor, lack of motivation and self-discipline have been identified as causes of the dilemma.

---

* See the U.S. Department of Labor's "Statistics on Manpower," March 1969.

The first contention, that blacks have only themselves to blame for occupying lower-rung jobs, lacks merit because it assumes that many opportunities for better jobs are available. But how many occupational opportunities really are available to them? Though this is changing, it is public knowledge that major unions and employers have stubbornly resisted opening their doors to blacks. This not only reduces the incentive to seek training but makes it impossible for those who have received training to obtain skilled jobs. Consequently, many blacks have jobs which do not require all their skills; in short, some remain poor despite their talents and training.

A college education poses financial obstacles that the average black family cannot overcome. Nor does a college education assure an escape from poverty. As many white students with college degrees, even advanced degrees, are learning, higher education offers little assurance of a secure and well-paid job. Job opportunities, even for the better educated, are drying up. Amazingly, the average (median) yearly earnings of black college graduates in metropolitan areas is about the same as white high school graduates.* The presumed lack of will among poor blacks to improve their earnings and occupations could be seen as a sensible refusal to nourish unrealistic ambitions.

Certainly, the lack of adequate opportunities for blacks —and this brings us to the second issue—accounts for a proportionately larger percentage being outside the labor force, neither employed nor seeking work. The lower-class culture theorists, however, attribute this to the lower-class culture of the poor, with its presumably large number of unmotivated individuals. There are indeed those in both the black and white communities who are poor and wanting but lack

---

* U.S. Bureau of the Census, "Trends in Social and Economic Conditions in Metropolitan Areas," Current Population Reports, Series P-23, No. 27, February 7, 1969.

an incentive to work. Their numbers however, are not as great as some assume.

The official statistics of the Department of Labor show recent periods when the percentage of civilian black adult males neither working nor seeking work was under 5 per cent. Even if we assume that the official figure reflected culturally induced indifference to work, the overwhelming majority were still either working or actively seeking work, and therefore not knocked out, so to speak, by the culture. In reality, the 5 per cent figure is a composite of many things. First, the Department of Labor uses a very strict criterion for determining whether persons not employed are actually seeking work. Individuals might not be meeting the technical criteria of the agency while in fact searching for jobs. More important, the Department of Labor excludes those who have not been seeking jobs because they do not believe work is available. According to the Department of Labor's own study, this group is so large that it would raise the unemployment rate by about 50 per cent; but it is included in the out-of-the-labor-force category. There are still others who, though indicating no desire to work in the first place, would quickly accept work if opportunities were regularly available. Clearly, the black male adults who need to work but are too apathetic to be reached by even the promise of stable, well-paid jobs are extremely few in number.

The structural argument, then, makes a great deal of sense. But granted that the poor need drastic improvements in objective conditions, the proponents of this view often do not fully consider how these changes are to be brought about. Certainly a hands-off policy, with its dependence upon the vagaries of the business cycle, has not eradicated poverty and slum conditions. On the other hand, government intervention has not proved to be a panacea, because many programs, whatever the intentions behind them, have been to the disadvantage of the poor. For example, urban renewal has uprooted large numbers of poor families, particularly blacks, from low rent housing, thus generating even greater poverty.

The road to improving conditions for the poor seems to run in one direction—toward the achievement of political power. Without political leverage to operate, negotiate, and form alliances, the poor will probably not be able to make demands that stand any chance of being met. Without shifting the balance of power, practices and policies that favor the poor will remain inadvertent, coincidental, and infrequent. "Power to the people," must become more than a slogan; the poor must build permanent political organizations.

If the central task is to organize for change, then the key questions are whether the poor can be organized and whether their leaders are capable of doing the job. To those who are convinced that the culture of poverty is altogether self-defeating and characterizes the poor in general, the answer must be No. This view, for example, is the main message in Michael Harrington's influential book on poverty, *The Other America*. Because the culture of poverty is both self-defeating and widespread, the middle class, he claims, must intervene on behalf of the poor.

But the record shows that the poor really can be organized, and the large-scale union organizing of poor workers during the Depression of the thirties is not the only evidence. More recently, poor farm workers have been organizing successfully against extremely powerful opposition, and many other poor people's organizations, such as welfare rights groups, public housing tenant unions, and senior citizens' groups have sprung up. Admittedly, organizing the poor is not easy. But there is no doubt that it can be done.

However, are not the leaders of more or less effective poor people's organizations generally middle-class? We have already noted the penchant of lower-class culture theorists to assume that the absence of certain failings—that is, failings according to middle-class standards—is evidence that a middle-class style has been adopted. Leaders of the poor, often characterized as middle-class, are those who are highly articulate spokesmen and generally seem better educated than their followers. They may display a wide range of other abilities, such as a knack for gaining the confidence of others. They may project that charm we call charisma. In their personal lives, many have attempted to improve their income and occupational status, and others have not; but in both cases their apparent abilities and talents tag them as upwardly mobile, which is interpreted to mean that their values are middle-class.

To interpret the existence of these abilities and presumed ambitions to improve themselves economically as evidence that these poor are joining the middle-class culture reflects a very narrow conception of lower-class culture. The poor, after all, have plenty of talented members, and the desire to earn more money is by no means a middle-class invention. Neither of these points, of course, should have to be made. To categorize certain virtues, if they are in fact virtues, as components of the middle-class style of life reveals what many already suspect—that the middle-class is ethnocentric.

Carefully comparing political styles of middle- and lower-class leaders generally reveals striking differences. Among many lower-class leaders, there is little or no concern with respectability. Confrontations with opponents do not embarrass them. They do not shy away from conflict. And they do not hesitate to use tactics that the establishment and public-at-large consider illegitimate. The major argument here is that, within the lower-class culture, there is a wide range of options, including positive ones, to draw upon. Not only can the poor be organized, but they can be organized by leaders whose own styles are decidedly lower-class. In fact, there is much to recommend some of the qualities encouraged by their culture. Not being concerned with respectability, they are not as readily amenable to co-optation by the establishment. Their continued militancy, in fact, may crucially depend upon their ability to resist the middle-class culture.

The NAC organizers could not be co-opted, which was certainly to their political credit. But they would not "sell out," in part, because in fact they had little to sell. They surrendered to those aspects of the lower-class culture that were most inimical to the development of political organization and power. Though the process in which conditions tend to generate certain modes of adaptation is very intricate, here in brief is what happens.

With few prospects of earning a stable, adequate living, many poor persons tend to become present-time-oriented and place great emphasis on gratifying immediate needs. They do not learn to plan because there seems to be nothing to plan for. This tendency to respond in terms of immediate needs shapes the rest of their behavior. Job insecurity generates family instability and a loss of personal pride. Consequently, some men flit about from one woman to another to obtain sexual favors and proof of their masculinity. Many lower-class men, whose relations to the labor force are marginal, tend to develop antagonism toward work itself. But having little or no money they cannot escape their vulnerability and hence dependency, which in turn generates a strong ambivalence toward authority. They feel at once strongly dependent upon authority and strongly antagonistic toward it.

Without resources of their own, they must still subsist; but having no resources, they have nothing to trade. Consequently, they have to manipulate others—put them on, as members of the lower-class themselves say. Some develop this into an art and gain many psychic and material gratifications from employing ruses. But most of the time their lives are filled with tedium and they are often depressed. This makes them especially eager to seize opportunities for excitement, of whatever sort may be available. Another major characteristic of lower-class men is a desire to be seen as brave, daring, and fearless. This posture is partly protective; that is, it is one appropriate response to a vulnerable life situation. The tough stance is also valued for fostering a sense of masculinity. Like other adaptations, it sometimes becomes valued for its own sake and serves as a source of gratification.

These patterned responses crystallize into a culture in which they become normative expectations, or at least are condoned and not frowned upon. Within any group adhering to these culture patterns, the significance of a specific norm may vary from one member to another. For some, a pattern becomes strongly internalized, while others adopt it only to achieve status and approval in the group.

The degree of internalization of lower-class culture patterns varied between the Rogers Point organizers. Jerry Cook and Curtis Jones seemed more psychologically pulled by the culture than the others. Eddie Daniels often gave the impression that he was riding along with the consensus, even enthusiastically, but that he would have been equally flexible playing other roles. George Franklyn seemed more capable of planning than the others and of having the capacity to modify his expressive style significantly. But like the others, he went along with the prevailing mood. None of the organizers would risk jeopardizing their status and approval by not conforming.

While the organizers differed from each other in the extent to which they internalized norms, the norms themselves also had varying priorities for each of them. Flouting authority did not seem to be a major concern to Jerry Cook; putting on others preoccupied him. At the same time, he greatly respected Curtis Jones for constantly defying the Housing Authority. Apparently the various prescriptions of lower-class culture, which largely directed NAC's political activities, represented a complicated integration of internalized norms and needs for status and approval.

Had the highly expressive character of the organizers' behavior been harnessed to serve the pursuit of long-range goals, several other important components of their lower-class style could have served productive ends. Toughness, as manifested in courage and a capacity for taking risks, is a real asset in political organizing. The gratifications of putting on others might have been found in shrewd manipulation and planning. Defiance of authority could have been expressed with dignity, as an assertion of principle. With their sights set on clear goals, the organizers might have been far more willing to endure hard work patiently.

Whether or not leaders, lower-class or otherwise, can exercise the necessary restraint and foresight is often a matter of delicate balance. The Rogers Point organizers could not. We have seen how the lack of various structural constraints encouraged their expressive behavior, and I have discussed the self-defeating consequences of their sectarian political style, which also fostered expressive behavior. The influence of the lower-class culture has already been spelled out. The personal backgrounds of Curtis Jones and George Franklyn, as expressed in their active mobility strivings, suggested that they had the capacity for planned action, but their actual political behavior did not confirm this. I strongly suspect that if George Franklyn had occupied the chief leadership role, the strike might have been more successful. But there is no way of proving this contention.

We do know that expressive political behavior spelled disaster for NAC's organizing efforts, and that it has been having similar consequences for other poor people's organizations. The hopeful sign is that leaders of the poor, like anyone else, are capable of learning from the political experiences of others. Those who do will be able to draw upon the most productive aspects of the cultural influences that have shaped them and their constituencies. These leaders will be a major force for social change because they will understand the urgency of building permanent poor people's organizations. They will be able to grasp the simple yet compelling principle that only organizing builds power.

A LOOK AT
MY FIELD
EXPERIENCE

The reporting of research findings is supposed to inform and illuminate, and perhaps dispel illusions, but it can sometimes create illusions of its own. Since the reader sees only the last of many drafts, and none of the hazards of the research itself, he may assume that every step of the research process has been taken in strict accordance with the canons of scientific inquiry. The researcher, indeed, is continuously trying to impose order upon chaos, and the culmination of his efforts in a written report should represent the triumph of order. But in shielding readers from the anarchy often inherent in his work, he obscures the extent to which his research efforts have been haphazard, and how his commitment to the scientific method may have been more a goal than an actual achievement.

This is particularly applicable to social science research, and most of all, to participation-observation field work. In studying an event as it naturally occurs, external controls are ruled out. Nevertheless, the researcher does employ various strategies to pursue his work systematically. In this Appendix I shall describe the various procedures I used in conducting my research. First, though, something should be said about the agony—I can think of no better term—that this kind of research can involve.

The rent strike at Rogers Point was a cluster of fast-breaking events. At any given moment many possibly significant things were happening. Perhaps lawyers were meeting, a striking tenant was defecting, and the organizers were being interviewed by newspaper reporters. None of these incidents would ever be repeated in exactly the same way. Once missed, they were lost, at least from my direct observation. I thus found myself frantically running from one place to another, nights as well as days and in various parts of the city.

Simply maintaining access to the organizers kept me in rapid motion. As a Caucasian researcher among black nationalists, and a man employed by an organization that they viewed with increasing suspicion, I was never really in a secure position. At times I was given the cold shoulder at their office, and on two occasions we argued and they virtually ostracized me. Moreover, even the lawyers who were employed by the Association were not always inclined to keep me informed. So besides chasing from one incident to another, I had to pursue my sources aggressively.

As events whirled around me I found few constants against which I could evaluate the actual significance of the seemingly inexhaustible number of variables. Even I was variable; both my thinking and my situation changed during the course of the strike. I had to make certain not to see changes in my own perceptions for changes in others. There were many other threats against my objectivity. To cite just one, my own feelings about the project became a potential hazard. I had to resist giving in to my own activist inclinations, and to make sure that I would not be overwhelmed emotionally by the difficulties of remaining on the sidelines most of the time. I also felt guilty about the critical turn my research was taking. In the beginning I had assumed that my account would be implicitly sympathetic to the organizers, and they did too. Only later did I become fully aware of how various non-political influences were adversely affecting the goals of the strike. At first I criticized some of the organizers' behavior and offered suggestions, but they always ignored my advice. I soon became less candid; the organizers were generally antagonistic to ideas from others, and I did not want to jeopardize the completion of my project. Nevertheless, on many occasions during the strike, my personal feelings were at war with my ideas of research standards.

In short, my research required me to bear with a high level of insecurity, disorganization, and anarchy. A strong interest in the problem was certainly a major incentive to seeing it through until it became, in my estimate, a coherent whole. But there was more at stake than the research enterprise itself. Bringing this project to a close represented a commitment to my personal unity as well. Because the project occupied most of my time and energy for over a year, it was almost as if the project and I were one. Because my research was fairly unstructured, I found it personally fragmenting. So in completing the project by making sense out of my data, I was also putting myself back together again; and that can never be a perfectly objective process.

II

There were three basic methodological problems that I had to deal with: selecting and defining a research problem; developing maximum access to the various participants of my study; and finding appropriate research techniques for gathering data. In choosing a problem, I was first influenced by the fact of having been employed as a sociologist for the City's Office of Economic Opportunity legal service program. The Association's decision to hire a sociologist reflected the interests of the organization's director, who was not only a lawyer but a sociologist as well. The responsibilities of my position had not really been defined except that the coordinator favored conducting some basic research on problems relating to the law and the poor.

I wanted to produce a manuscript on an interesting and important problem, and the coordinator and I agreed that for the first month I should explore areas that would be worth researching. During this exploratory period, I began to take on several other functions. Various lawyers in the organization would come to me for social data to buttress their legal cases, and my research department, which included two research assistants, worked closely with the lawyers in developing legal case material.

Because I had considerable political experience and contacts in the City working with community organizations, I began to serve another function, which neither the director nor I had anticipated when I was hired. The Association was eager to represent organizational clients, believing that organizations could provide lawyers with socially significant cases. I acted as a bridge between various organizational clients and the Association. For example, I established and helped sustain contact between the law firm and a community organization for the purpose of halting a major redevelopment project. My department was also instrumental in gathering social data for the case.

All these activities enhanced my access to the Association's lawyers, whose cooperation was important for my research. When they learned about my research interests they would voluntarily provide me with important information and invite me to key meetings. However, acting as a bridge between the Association and various community organizations was not to be considered part of my own research project. There was no expectation that I would be responsible for handling communication problems that might develop between the Association and the clients I selected for my study.

The group that I eventually decided to study was one of several organizational clients who sought legal service from the Association. Legal action was being taken by the Housing Authority to compel tenants to pay their rents or face eviction proceedings, and the Rogers Point organizers sought the assistance of the Association to prevent evictions.

At first, I intended to study only the relationship between these organizers and their white professional lawyers, a relationship which was beset with problems and tensions from the very beginning. I thought that their ability to work together could have relevance for improving the conditions of the poor, which was one of the major reasons I wanted to pursue this subject. Also, the kind of problems that developed between them engaged my curiosity. It frequently seemed to me that the lawyers and the blacks came from different worlds, so often did they seem to misinterpret each other. However, I eventually decided that studying the interaction between them would be only one aspect of my research. My focus of study broadened to investigating other dimensions of the organizers' political behavior. I became interested in learning not only how they related to the lawyers but how they behaved toward others, such as the tenants and the Housing Authority. The initial impetus for considering this shift was my rare opportunity as a Caucasian researcher to study the political operation of a black militant organization and to learn something about how they made political decisions.

I discussed my interest in expanding the research project with the Association's director, who happily encouraged me to do so. I was working long hours performing a variety of functions for the Association, and so the coordinator did not interpret the reformulation of my research interests as deflecting from my work commitments to the organization. He also believed that a better understanding of how organizers related to lawyers would be gained by evaluating how they functioned with other individuals and groups. I later realized that there was much more truth to this position than I had originally suspected. By comparing how they related to various groups, I soon learned that some of their difficulties with the Association lawyers could not be explained, as I had first believed, as essentially a response to being misunderstood by middle class white professionals who thought that they knew better. In short, the comparative method was useful even for understanding the specific relations between the organizers and the lawyers. But most important, by investigating what the organizers thought about and how they related to various incumbents, I was able to learn a great deal about what structured and motivated their political behavior.

Of course, my research depended upon having adequate access to the organizers. Though this posed problems throughout most of the study, they were not insurmountable ones. Initial access to the group was readily obtained simply by my being employed by the Association. I was able to attend all meetings between the organizers and the lawyers, and when tenants were brought to court for trial, as they were over a period of several months, I was able to engage the organizers, who always came along with the tenants, in conversation. Before the court proceedings began I could talk with them about their situation and also listen to the discussions that frequently ensued between the lawyers, tenants, and organizers.

The lawyers referred to me as their researcher, who assisted in gathering material needed for the preparation for their legal suits. This introduction gave me a basis for visiting NAC's office to talk with the organizers, who already knew me through the various political activities I had engaged in before accepting a position with the Association. After several visits to their office, I told them that I was also engaging in a research project to evaluate how lawyers and organizers are able to work together, and so I was especially interested in learning how they and the lawyers related to each other. My research interests did not make the organizers defensive or suspicious. It always seemed to them that the lawyers, not themselves, were required to prove their moral integrity and demonstrate that they had progressive political principles.

I listened carefully during this early period, but as I wanted to learn more about their attitudes, and as my research interests shifted to studying their overall political behavior rather than just how they related to the lawyers, I needed further access to the group. I wanted to be in a position to attend their meetings, engage them in a wide range of conversations, feel free to visit and spend considerable time around their office, and have them keep me informed of various public meetings they would be attending where they expected to play an active role.

Though the Association provided me with my initial contact, my position as one of their employees could have undermined my research because the organizers grew increasingly antagonistic toward the organization. It did at first create some problems, but in the long run the access I achieved and the confidence I gained increased, though the bond between the Association and NAC tended to remain fragile and explosive. I enjoyed two advantages. I had been formerly involved in several political battles against various public agencies in the City, and was best known for playing a leading role in fighting against the approval of a redevelopment project. In fact, I had publicly debated the redevelopment agency's executive director at a meeting in their neighborhood, which they had attended. So the organizers knew about me and the kind of role I had been playing before I joined the Association. They realized that on many issues we were political allies. Although they were very suspicious of Caucasians, I was regarded as one the better whites around the City.

The hard work of establishing close rapport with the organizers was still ahead. I knew, though, that even during the SNCC purge of white liberals in 1966, some whites were retained for their technical skills. I decided to offer them mine. This was consistent with my political principles because I believed that the tenants' grievances were generally legitimate, that the Housing Authority should alter many of its practices, and that building poor people's organizations was essential. As time passed, I became in effect a research assistant for the organizers. I brought them various public documents, checked out legal issues for them, helped one of the organizers establish a settlement house in the community by participating in the writing of a proposal (which was eventually funded), and otherwise attempted to find out whatever they wanted to know.

I soon developed close ties with three of the organizers. Though the group's leader seemed to like me, I always got the feeling that my being Caucasian troubled him. However, my usefulness to the organization tended to ease tensions. One consequence of the close relationships we developed was their willingness to talk to me about their personal lives. Of course, I was always an outsider whose presence was contingent upon their good graces. But after a while I could visit their office frequently and spend several hours sitting around as the various organizers and other individuals came in and out.

I also established contact with the Housing Authority,

which may seem surprising in view of my close relationship with the organizers. Ironically, this became possible because my employment with the Association brought me into contact with the Housing Authority. One of the administrators appeared in court as a witness for the Authority. We met there and I subsequently visited him at his office. We chatted often and became fairly friendly. He provided me with data and showed me Housing Authority records that were relevant to my research interests. Through him I met other administrators of the Housing Authority staff, including the manager of the Rogers Point Project, who enjoyed meeting and talking with me about Housing Authority problems. Having established relationships with all sides in the political controversy gave me ample opportunity to gather whatever data I needed.

The following situations provided the main sources for gathering data. First, I attended many formally scheduled meetings, both private and public, to which the organizers were invited, called on their own, or crashed. These included meetings with the lawyers, administrative staff members representing the Housing Authority, public officials, and organizations in their community. Second, I had many informal discussions with the organizers, collectively and individually, either at their office or elsewhere, such as in a cafe or a bar. Third, I observed how they related when informally brought into contact with each other as well as with other citizens in the City. Fourth, one of the organizers with whom I became quite friendly kept me informed. I learned through him a great deal about how the organizers related to and felt about each other, and also how decisions were made. He was able to corroborate what I had already learned, and alerted me to issues that I had not been aware of. Fifth, I interviewed virtually all the striking tenants, mostly about their situation in public housing and their attitudes toward the strike. Finally, I spoke to various people about the organizers; these included public officials, community leaders, both radicals and moderates, and lawyers at the Association. These discussions helped me check my own impressions and stimulated my thinking about them.

I behaved in different ways in these various settings. I think Herbert Gans' categories for clarifying the role of the researcher in terms of differences in his actual behavior is useful here.* He noted three different types. First is the researcher who acts as observer, physically present at an event but not really participating in it. Second is the researcher who participates, but only as researcher, with his participation determined by his research interests rather than by the roles required in the situation he is studying. Third is the researcher who temporarily abdicates his study role and becomes a real participant.

I generally related to the organizers in the first two roles. Quite often, at the scheduled meetings and informal discussions they engaged in among themselves at their office, I was able to limit myself to the observer role. I even obtained important data simply by listening to phone conversations they received and made. I learned, for example, that when the group's leader, Curtis Jones, would be speaking to the other party somewhat impatiently and even condescendingly, it was often a tenant. So by simply visiting their office and observing, I obtained important clues to how the organizers related to the striking tenants as well as to other interested parties in the rent strike.

I acted as a participating researcher by frequently asking questions or making statements to see what responses would be given. These were in no sense formal interviews;

* Herbert Gans, *The Urban Villagers* (New York, 1964), pp. 338–339.

I did not explicitly say that my line of questioning reflected my research interests. Whether I decided to play this role or only observe was often a matter of using my instincts. As time progressed I felt more relaxed about asking questions and otherwise participating as a researcher.

My role as an actual participant was minimal because I wanted to avoid influencing the behavior of the organizers. Fortunately, this fitted their view of what my role should be, both as a Caucasian and an outsider. I had had many opportunities to witness their extremely adverse reaction to advice or criticism, even when it was offered by "outsiders" who sympathized with their goals. Their reaction was often serious enough to jeopardize their relationships with those who, as they put it, "think they know better." Accordingly, they thought better of me for not interfering in their affairs.

There were two kinds of situations, however, in which I played the participant role. Though the expectations of the organizers and my own research interests usually kept my involvement as a participant minimal, sometimes my activist inclinations overcame my research aims. I really did want to see the organizers win concessions from the Housing Authority, and there were times when I really thought they were missing the boat. So occasionally I spoke up. Fortunately, I knew them well enough to sense how to raise issues without offending them. In any case, they never took my advice. On a few other occasions, I was forced into the participant role. At some small meetings between the organizers and the lawyers, for example, my opinion was sometimes asked for, and I felt obliged to say what I actually thought.

When my involvement extended beyond my research interests, I recorded these experiences and included some description of the possible impact my role might have had. Actually, my advice was rarely sought or offered. Much more serious was dealing with my own feelings about how the strike was being handled by the organizers, so I also took notes on how I personally reacted to the experiences I was writing about. This later made it easier to achieve a fairly detached perspective. But it would be wrong to imply that my sensibilities were always stumbling blocks to my research. Without a considerable emotional investment in the cause of the strike, I doubt that I could have written this book.